Golf

The Science & The Art

Golf

The Science & The Art

Leon Z. Seltzer

TATE PUBLISHING & Enterprises

Golf: The Science and the Art
Copyright © 2007 by Leon Z. Seltzer. All rights reserved.

This title is also available as a Tate Out Loud product. Visit www.tatepublishing.com for more information.

The opinions expressed by the author are not necessarily those of Tate Publishing, LLC.

Published by Tate Publishing & Enterprises, LLC
127 E. Trade Center Terrace | Mustang, Oklahoma 73064 USA
1.888.361.9473 | www.tatepublishing.com

Tate Publishing is committed to excellence in the publishing industry. The company reflects the philosophy established by the founders, based on Psalms 68:11,
"The Lord gave the word and great was the company of those who published it."

Book design copyright © 2007 by Tate Publishing, LLC. All rights reserved.
Cover design by Geneveive Stotler
Interior design by Steven Jeffrey

Published in the United States of America

ISBN: 978-1-60247-848-0
1. Sports: Golf: Instruction
07.10.09

CONTENTS

THE AUTHOR

Golf has been a huge part of my life. I feel that I should include something about myself and how I became the "golf nut" I was and still am as the prelude to what is to follow. It wasn't always easy, but I wouldn't trade my experience and the life I led for anything else. I am so grateful that I have been fortunate enough to live through almost all of the twentieth century.

As a vocation I chose aeronautical engineering, which later became aerospace engineering. During my four and one-half decades of involvement, the field I worked in went from wire braced biplanes, in which I learned to fly, to putting a man on the moon. One of the students I taught became the flight director for NASA during the exciting space race that included the Apollo program. For my avocation, I chose golf and immediately became an addict. I lived through the growth of golf from Bobby Jones to Tiger Woods by way of Jack Nicklaus, and from Glenna Collett to Michelle Wie by way of Mickey Wright. How lucky can one man be? (Though I do regret that I did not have the opportunity to see Joyce Wethered play.)

I can't remember why I fell in love with golf shortly after I learned how to spell the word "golf." It must be true love because it has lasted for more than eighty years. Over this period of time my involvement with the game has covered just about all of its aspects: playing, reading, collecting and consulting. Now that I am in my nineties, I can look back and appreciate how much pleasure I derived from golf and wonder what I would have done without it. I was lucky to have a good golf game to enjoy, because I was pretty much a self-taught player, except for the little there was available to read at that time.

Evidently, I was able to recognize the right elements to incorporate into my golf swing, because my game held up over all the years I played golf. I don't recall having ever been in a slump during all that time. When I was 85 years old, in successive weeks I shot 75 and 74, ten and eleven strokes under my age on our par 72 country club course. I will share some of my insights on the important elements of a good golf swing in the chapter, "Golf Swing Fundamentals."

I believe that I was originally turned on to the sport by all the stories about Bobby Jones during the late 1920s. Since I was raised in the central part of Chicago, I never had a chance to caddy or play when I was a boy. Golf ball driving ranges did not exist at that time. One of my older sisters did play a little golf, but the arrival of the depression soon put an end to that. However, that didn't stop me from going out into our back yard and swinging her clubs whenever I had an opportunity.

One of the elements of the golf swing that I recognized immediately was the importance of keeping the head still during the entire swing. In order to teach myself to do this I devised a gadget made from one of my mother's hose. This was before panty hose came into being. I made a stocking cap from the top part of one of the stockings and tied a light cord to the top where I had gathered it together. I tossed the cord over a tree limb in the back yard. By trial and error, I adjusted the cord until it was straight and vertical when my head was in the address position. With this training aid in position on my head, I practiced my golf swing. If my head moved to the left, right or down during the swing, the stocking cap would come off. It took a lot of time and a lot of patience but I did learn to execute a golf swing, from address position to the end of the follow through, without having the stocking cap dislodge.

From the onset, I was interested in the mechanics of the golf swing. My fascination with the "why" and "how" about all things must be the reason I finally chose engineering as a career. This turned out to be one of the best decisions I ever made.

Before the depression hit, my family spent some summers at a cottage on the beach near Michigan City, Indiana. On weekdays the beach was deserted during the early morning hours. Every morning I would take a mashie and hit golf balls off the sand. This practice taught me to hit the ball first when swinging an iron. I am quite sure that this was a factor in my good iron play later on. The old time professionals referred to what I did as "squeezing the ball between the club face and the ground."

The depression hit my family very hard. As a result, I went to work after school before I was thirteen, and this kept me from doing much in the way of golf or any other extra-curricular activities, for that matter. Finally, around 1930, a lighted driving range opened about a half-mile from our home and the drug store where I worked nights. The driving range stayed open until about 1:00 a.m., which gave me a chance to hit a bucket or two of balls after I finished work at the drug store.

Since we had moved by this time, I didn't have a tree to use for my training aid. Instead, I used a mirror that was located over the mantle in our living room. Looking in the mirror, I could line up my head with a spot on the wall behind me and swing away. As I looked in the mirror during the swing, I was able to concentrate on keeping my head still and this worked as well as the stocking cap.

I played my first game of golf at a nine-hole golf course in Jackson Park when I was fourteen. Jackson Park was located across the street from the high school I attended. I broke 50 in my first attempt. Back then, I used hickory-shafted clubs. I recall that the first steel-shafted club I owned was a MacGregor "Bap" brassie. At least I was off and running, even if not very fast. Both my after-school work and the depression of the 1930s kept me from doing very much in the way of golf other than swinging a golf club, but I did continue to do that. In addition, I read everything about golf that I could lay my hands on.

Because of the depression, I could not afford to go away to an engineering college at that time to study aeronautical engineering. Since I had been working in drug stores from the time I was thirteen, and I had a pretty good job working evenings at that time. Since my days were free, I enrolled at the University of Illinois College of Pharmacy, which was located in Chicago. Before the end of my sophomore year, I took the State Board examination for assistant registered pharmacist and passed it on my first attempt. This helped me financially until I received my pharmacy degree. Two years later I finally enrolled at the University of Michigan in the aeronautical engineering program. To make ends meet I worked as a pharmacist at the University Health Service. Winning three academic scholarships at Michigan was a big financial help, too.

During the summer of 1937, I worked in a drug store that was located in the Congress Hotel in Chicago. There was a professional golf tournament held in Chicago during that summer, and four of the players that I recognized stayed at the hotel during the tournament. One was Ralph Guldhal, the U.S. Open champion, who stayed there with his wife. They were very friendly people and I was thrilled to visit with both of them on several occasions during that week. Harry Cooper was another person who was easy to be with. I had several conversations with him about photography, which was his hobby. I had the feeling that Cooper worked at golf for a living because the depression interfered with any other plans he might have had. Since this was before television sent the purses skyrocketing, it was easy to understand. I will touch on that later.

The other two players I recognized were Gene Sarazen and Jimmy Thompson. Neither of them were very friendly, and it was difficult to get into a conversation with them. After watching the genial Sarazen on "Shell's Wonderful World of Golf," I wanted to ask the real Gene Sarazen to stand up. Thompson was a steady customer for Gauztex self-adhesive bandage. The golf club grips that were in use at that time were made of wrapped, smooth calfskin. These could become slick quite easily, so Thompson wrapped his grips with an overlay of the Gauztex bandage to give them a tacky feeling. I tried this myself and since I tend to have very dry skin I liked it very much.

While I was at the University of Michigan studying for my engineering degree, I continued to work to support myself. Consequently, the only chance I had to play the fine University of

Michigan golf course was during holiday breaks when most of the students were away. After I earned my engineering degree I accepted a position with Douglas Aircraft Company in Santa Monica, California, where I worked as a design criteria engineer. I left Douglas three months before the Pearl Harbor attack to accept a teaching position at Virginia Tech in Blacksburg, Virginia. During World War II, I spent most of my time teaching engineering to military personnel who were part of the Army Specialized Training Program. What with the war time accelerated programs and no vacations during that period, my golf was, again, put on hold. This continued through a good part of the early post-war period because of the return of the veterans who took advantage of the G.I. Bill of Rights. The accelerated program continued with teaching overloads and large classes.

In 1949, I left Virginia Tech and moved to Morgantown, West Virginia, to accept a position as Professor and Chairman of the Department of Aeronautical Engineering at West Virginia University. The aeronautical engineering enrollment was fairly low when I started. As a result, for the first time since I was twelve years old I had some time for myself. Morgantown Country Club was less than two miles from both my home and my office. I joined the club before our furniture arrived. Now I had time to play golf and practice as much as I wanted to, and I did. I had a golf club in my hand seven days a week, and it paid off. By 1952, my handicap was zero. This put me in elite company since only one other member at the club played to scratch. At this point in time, our club was using the Calkins system for handicapping. I am not sure what my handicap would have been under the current system, where the slope rating of the golf course is used. There were times when I was not at all happy with the Calkins system of handicapping. I recall one time during the club handicap tournament when I lost a match 5 and 3. When this match ended on the 15th green, I was three under par. I was playing a high handicapper, and I lost two holes which I had birdied. Later, handicap tournaments were broken up into flights in order to avoid matches such as this.

I had an unfortunate, but interesting, experience during one winter and learned a valuable lesson from it. We had a severe winter that year and the golf course was shut down for some time. In my frustration, I went to the university field house where they had a golf driving net set up and hit balls in the net. I continued to do this, almost daily, for quite some time until the weather improved. Finally, the snow disappeared and the golf course was re-opened. Since the club did not have a driving range or practice area available, I just started to play. My first tee shot had the most horrendous duck hook I have ever seen, before or since. I had a devil of a time curing that hook. It had become a real habit. Never again did I use an indoor net for practice or exercise.

It was in 1953 that I decided to enter my first 72-hole stroke play competition. The Preston Country Club in Kingwood, West Virginia, hosted a tri-state golf tournament primarily for amateur players from West Virginia, Maryland and Pennsylvania. As the time for the tournament approached, I started to think about the difference between stroke play and match play. Almost all of our club tournaments had been conducted using a match play format. I now realized that whatever I did on the first tee would stay with me until the tournament was over. In match play, it doesn't make any difference if you lose a hole by one stroke or four. In stroke play, you carry your foul balls with you as baggage all the way to the bottom of the cup on the 72nd green. I don't recall ever having been as nervous as I was on the first tee that Friday morning of the first day of the tournament. The first hole was a 595-yard par 5. I hit two fairly good woods and then hit a pitching wedge into the hole for an eagle 3. What a start! On the 165-yard ninth hole, I hit a five iron into the hole for an ace, finishing the nine with a 33, despite a double bogey along the way. After the hole-in-one, I made 26 pars on the next 27 holes. My only bogey in those 27 holes was the result of a three putt green. On that hole, there was a large piece of dirt on my ball. The rules in effect in 1953 did not permit a golfer to clean his ball after reaching the putting surface and as a result I missed a fairly short putt.

After the tri-state tournament, I knew that I was a golfer. I could play in stroke play tournaments without choking, even on and around the greens. My short game was good enough that on occasions, when I was faced with a dangerous shot to the green as a result of a drive that was miss hit or not well placed, I would aim to miss the green intentionally on the safe side because I was confident that I could get the ball up and down. I did this several times during the tri-state tournaments on the par 4 third hole, if I didn't hit my drive close enough to where I was aiming. That was the water hole I had double bogeyed on the first day of my first tournament. On the morning of the last day of the 1953 tournament, just before I teed off, one of the spectators came up to me and asked for my autograph. This was the first and last time that I was ever asked for my autograph on a golf course. I had to laugh at this and I believe that I was more relaxed when I arrived at the first tee, but it also gave my confidence a significant boost. I ended up finishing third in my first stroke play event.

GOLF AND GOLF IMMORTALS

During my active golf life I have had the good fortune of meeting or being around a number of golf celebrities. It was always interesting even if I was not always pleased with what I saw. I am happy to say that a large majority of the celebrities were and are people I was happy to know. This was just as true for the "big names" as for those who were not famous.

My earliest contacts were mentioned in the previous chapter. I met Ralph Guldahl, Harry Cooper, Gene Sarazen and Jimmy Thompson at the Congress Hotel in Chicago in 1937. I surely would have loved to have had more time with both Guldahl and Cooper.

In 1953 I spent the entire U.S. Open week in Pittsburgh when the tournament was played at Oakmont. That was a very severe test of golf at that time. Back then, the sand in the bunkers at Oakmont was raked with a deeply saw-toothed rake which left triangular furrows that were the better part of three inches deep. I recall a particularly remarkable golf shot made by Joe Turnesa during that tournament. His ball came to rest in the rough on the very edge of the grass near a very deep bunker. Turnesa had to stand in the bunker with the ball about shoulder high. His golf swing was horizontal. I still cannot figure out how he could compensate for the loft on his club. Nevertheless, he hit a beautiful golf shot, truly remarkable. Turnesa came from a large family of boys, and all of them were excellent golfers. One of his brothers smoked a pipe, and kept this large curved pipe in his mouth when hitting his golf shots. Most of the Turnesa boys remained amateur golfers.

Before golf tournaments were televised the number of spectators at tournaments was quite small. Consequently, there weren't any ropes, marshals or other spectator controls that we have today. This changed with the U.S. Open in 1954 when the Open was televised for the first time. Until the 1954 U.S. Open, the spectators walked right along with the players until they reached the putting surface. What a pleasure it was to be able to hear the players comments and, sometimes, even their shot planning. This spoiled me for later tournaments. When I finally had to resort to using a periscope I gave up fighting the crowd. Now we have a number of new "stadium" type golf courses, which improve the viewing around the putting greens for the spectators. We also learned to have stands for the spectators from the British, who have always used them during their Open Tournaments. I saw them for the first time at Royal Lytham and St. Annes in 1969. Before tournaments were televised it was customary for the players to play 18 holes each of the first two days of the tournament and 36 holes on the final day.

A humorous incident occurred on the fifteenth tee during one of the rounds of the 1953 U.S. Open. I was walking with the group that included Sam Snead. Snead's group was waiting for the group ahead to get out of range when Cary Middlecoff walked up to where Snead was standing and said, "Sam, I picked up on the fourteenth tee." Snead looked at Middlecoff and drawled, "What's the matter, Doc, did you have a bad lie?"

Whenever I think about staying behind the ball during the golf swing, a picture of Middlecoff's swing comes to mind. Middlecoff and young Johnny Miller stayed behind the ball longer than anyone else that I ever watched. They both had the extreme "reverse C" finishes. I do not believe that the human body was ever meant to be subjected to that; in other words, I was envious.

On the last day of the 1953 U.S. Open, Porky Oliver shot 83 during the morning round. Porky was always fun to be around. He was such a good-natured person. When he teed off on the first hole of the afternoon round, he hit a beautiful towering drive right down the center of the fairway. He turned to the spectators around the tee and exclaimed, "Now, does that look like someone who shot 83 this morning?"

Back in the days of Snead, Hogan and Nelson (mostly before TV), the purses and winners' shares were so small that when I think of it now I can hardly believe that I am reporting accurately. Quite often tournament purses were $5000, with the winner's share a mere $500. In 1957, Dick Mayer received $7,200 for winning the U.S. Open and Doug Ford took home $8,750 for winning the Masters Tournament at Augusta. During this period there was Monday morning qualifying for players who were not well established. They were referred to as rabbits. These players drove from tournament to tournament and tried to qualify each Monday. Many did not make it and had to wait a week to try again.

The first breakthrough in golf tournament purses can be contributed to George S. May of Chicago. He was responsible for several innovations in professional golf tournaments. When in 1954 he offered a purse which provided $50,000 to the winner it astounded the golf world. That was at least five times what the winner earned in any other event, including the majors. One year Dick Mayer received $50,000 for winning May's "World Championship" but only $7,200 for winning the U.S. Open. In addition to the $50,000 first prize, the winner of May's tournament was guaranteed a series of ten golf exhibitions, which included a round of golf with three members of the golf club where the exhibition took place. He received $5,000 for each of the exhibitions. Here is an idea of what the top players earned during the early days before the PGA Tour existed. In 1938, Snead shattered the season earnings record with $19,534. The following year, Henry Picard was the leading money winner, and his winnings for the year were $10,303. Now, compare that with Tiger Woods earning $10,628,024 in 2002. Woods earned 1031 times as much as Picard! And that does not include endorsements, which may be as much as eight to ten times tournament earnings.

George May is responsible for the first televised broadcast of a golf event. He also introduced golf carts for the use of the members at Tam O'Shanter. His course had a telephone at each tee. Of course, this was long before cell phones were introduced. A story was circulated that Mr. May introduced a new feature requiring players to have their names pinned to their shirt backs for spectator recognition. It was reported that Ben Hogan refused to go along with this. Mr. May was adamant, and Hogan didn't play. Now caddies wear the names of their players.

I played the Tam O'Shanter golf course on a number of occasions with my brother, who was a member. One year, when I was ready to hit my second shot over the water to the 18th green, I noticed a small monument in the fairway ahead of me. When I inquired about this unusual sight, I was told that the monument marked the spot from which Lew Worsham holed an iron shot for an eagle to win the Tam O'Shanter tournament in 1953. This same tournament was the first to be shown on TV, and it is reported that George May actually paid the American Broadcasting Company to televise the event.

While I was a member of the Morgantown, West Virginia, Country Club an exhibition was scheduled at our club with the Bauer sisters, Marlene and Alice. Marlene was sixteen at the time. The older Alice was tiny. In order to get distance, she used a backswing that was so long the shaft was nearly vertical at the end of her backswing. I doubt that she weighed 100 pounds, and she was as cute as a button. Some spectators had difficulty watching her swing because they were fascinated by the safety pin at the back of the tight shorts she was wearing. Everyone wondered if it was going to hold during her very athletic swing.

I tried to take advantage of seeing Sam Snead every time it was possible for me to do so. I was successful on a number of occasions during the fourteen years that I was at West Virginia University. During that time, Snead was attached to the Greenbrier Resort at White Sulfur Springs in the southern part of the state. Snead had the best looking golf swing I have ever seen, before or since. Among my golf collector items, I had a sixteen millimeter film of Snead hitting various golf shots and playing. I watched it over and over again. The film had one scene where Snead was faced with a trouble shot. His golf ball was right next to a tree, but on the wrong side of it. He turned an eight iron over and played the shot left-handed. His left-handed swing was a mirror image of his regular swing and he hit a beautiful draw shot onto the putting surface. I recall Snead saying that when he needed added distance, he merely took the club back a little farther. He never tried to put any extra effort into his swing. This made a lot of sense since it provided a longer distance over which to accelerate the clubhead.

One of the times that I played in the West Virginia Open, it was held at Lakeview C.C. near Morgantown, West Virginia. Snead entered the tournament, as he did most of the time when he could fit the West Virginia State Open into his schedule. On Saturday, the second day of the tournament, my starting time was two groups ahead of Snead's. Just as I was finished hitting practice balls to my caddy, Snead arrived and took the space next to mine. I stood there and talked with Sam as he went through his routine, starting with the wedge and going up through his bag of clubs, including the driver. His caddy merely moved back every time Snead changed to another club. The caddy never had to move left or right to reach for a ball except for a one iron shot that went about fifteen feet to the caddy's right. I have never seen an exhibition like the one Snead put on that morning.

This was the first time that Snead had ever seen the Lakeview C.C. course, which was designed by J.G. Harrison. It was one of the most demanding courses I have ever played, the course having been cut out of virgin woods. Almost all of the fairways were thirty yards wide. There was a few feet of rough on each side and then trees lined every hole. When members rode in golf cars, they would also take forecaddies with them to spot the balls that went into the trees. In spite of the difficulty of the Lakeview layout, it was not unheard of for a visitor who was playing the course for the first time to do fairly well. The next time though, that same visitor would usually have a much, repeat much, higher score. The reason for this was that now that they had seen the course they knew where all the trouble was located and tried to steer the ball. Lakeview C.C. was in the Pittsburgh PGA District. For pro-am events at Lakeview C. C., most of the professionals came from the Pittsburgh area. Among them was Lew Worsham from Oakmont. The first year Lew played the course he did quite well, shooting 71. The next year his score was 83.

There was quite a bit of betting among the members, before the 54-hole State Open, on how Snead would fare since he had never seen the course before and had not played a practice round. On Friday, Snead shot 68 and was leading by several strokes. On Saturday, after just a few holes, the tournament was rained out. The betting on what Snead would shoot Sunday was very active. The members remembered what had happened to Worsham. The rain held off, and we were able to play on Sunday. Samuel Jackson Snead shot another 68. This particular event took place shortly after Snead had won thirteen straight weeks on a television program called All-Star Golf. He was undefeated when the series ended that year. Snead won almost everything there was to win, some several times, except for the USGA National Open. He won the Greater Greensboro Open a record eight times.

Later in this book I will discuss gamesmanship. I believe there is a prime example of gamesmanship of which Snead was the victim. This was during the 1947 U.S. Open that was played at the St. Louis Country Club. Snead and Lew Worsham ended up on the 72nd green all even, each of them approximately three feet from the hole. Seeing that he was away, Snead prepared to putt. After lining up the putt, and just as he was about to start his stroke, Worsham said, "Sam, I think that I'm away." Of course, Snead stopped, moved away from his ball and an official was called. The official confirmed that Snead was away. Snead went back to his ball, missed the short putt and lost the U.S. Open championship. That's gamesmanship.

In 1970, the U.S. Open was held at the new Hazeltine National Golf Club in Chaska, Minnesota. Tony Jacklin won the tournament by seven strokes. Before the tournament started, when Dave Hill was asked what the course lacked, he replied," "Eight acres of corn and a few cows." He was fined $150 for his comment. However, he wasn't alone in his judgment. In the first round, which was played in high winds, Palmer shot a 79, Gary Player an 80 and Nicklaus an 81. I always enjoyed watching Dave Hill play. He was such a great shot maker, as was Tommy Bolt, another feisty character.

It is somewhat amusing to see today's tour players with all the advertising that they wear, or display, when they are playing. For some, the money they get from this advertising and endorsements far exceeds their income from the golf tournaments. I believe it all started back about 1960. At that time, Gene Littler and some others began wearing caps with the name "Amana" on them. For this, they received $50 for each tournament where they wore the cap.

One of the tournaments played during the early years, from the late 1930s to the early 1950s, was the Goodall Round Robin Invitational. The sponsor, Goodall, was the maker of the famous Palm Beach line of clothes. This tournament had an unusual format. The field was limited to sixteen players, and each player had an opportunity to play against every other player. The scoring was done on the basis of how each player did in his group of four, each day, compared to the others in his group. It was a fun tournament to watch. Goodall produced 16mm films of this tournament, and made them available for group showings. On one occasion, as a slide show, the players tried to hit helium-filled balloons, which were anchored out on the practice range. It was surprising how many of the players did break balloons.

The Ryder cup matches were played at Old Warson Country Club in St. Louis in 1971. This was only a mile or so from my home when I was Dean at St. Louis University. I was fortunate enough to be one of the sponsors. At that time, the Ryder Cup matches were still being played between golfers from the United States and those of Great Britain. It was a real treat for me and my son, Tom, to meet the members of both teams at the welcoming dinner. Included on the American team that year were Jack Nicklaus, Arnold Palmer, Lee Trevino, Gene Littler and Billy Casper. The British group included Tony Jacklin, Peter Oosterhuis, who is now announcing in this country, Bernard Gallacher, and Christy

O'Connor. The captains were Jay Hebert for the USA and Eric Brown for the British.

On the day the tournament was about to start, Gene Littler, a class act, felt that his game wasn't sharp enough and he did not want to handicap the team. He evidently asked Jay Hebert not to use him during the first day. Gene spent the entire day on the practice tee, mostly working on his short game.

During the later years that the Ryder Cup matches were played between the U.S. and Great Britain, the Americans won almost every time. As a result the format was changed to include players from all of Europe. Since then most of the matches have been very close and more exciting to watch. After that, the President's Cup between the U.S. and the rest of the world except Europe and Great Britain, was initiated and played every other year, the years when the Ryder Cup matches were not played.

One of the extra treats I enjoyed during the 1971 Ryder Cup was meeting Henry Longhurst, the extraordinary English writer. You may remember Longhurst when he was a golf announcer for CBS at the Masters Tournaments from 1966 to 1973. Longhurst wrote a weekly column for the London Times for forty years. Some of his quotes have been used and repeated many times. Among them:

"Playing golf is like learning a foreign language."

"They say practice makes perfect. Of course it doesn't. For the vast majority of golfers it merely consolidates imperfection."

"If you call on God to improve the results of a shot while it is still in motion, you are using an outside agency and subject to appropriate penalties under the rules of golf."

You can't do much better than that.

While I was living in Clayton, Missouri, and employed as a Dean at St. Louis University, the PGA Tour initiated an event that was played at my club, Norwood Hills C.C., for the benefit of the Children's Hospital. Lee Trevino won it one of the two years that the event was held. For some reason, the event was not the financial success that was expected, and it was abandoned. The following year Hale Irwin initiated a pro-am event for the benefit of the same Children's Hospital. The Irwin event was not open to the general public. The spectators were only those invited by the amateur contestants, friends of the commercial sponsors and members of Old Warson C.C., where Hale was a member. Irwin's event produced more money for the Children's Hospital than the PGA event held the two previous years. I played in Hale's tournament for several years before I retired in 1981. The event was a one-day affair, held on Monday when the course was not open for play to the members of Old Warson. This was the same course that was used for the 1971 Ryder Cup. The membership at Old Warson was most generous in allowing their course to be used, frequently for such charitable purposes, as well as a qualifying venue for some USGA tournaments.

The professionals playing in the Hale Irwin event were about equally divided between the PGA Tour professionals and the Gateway Section PGA professionals. The latter group was com posed of the metropolitan St. Louis golf club professionals, which included some from neighboring Illinois cities. Several times the pro-am included a player from the Ladies Professional Golf Association. On one occasion I had the pleasure of having lunch with Nancy Lopez. Did I say pleasure? I meant delight. What a wonderful lady. We also had Donna Caponi, Marlene Floyd and Carol Mann, every one of them personable and gracious. One year, President Ford was there. What a nice person he was.

Among the touring pros that played in Hale's tournament were local favorites Jay Haas, Larry Ziegler, and Bob Goalby. Others included Don January, Larry Nelson, Mark O'Meara, Curtis Strange, Tommy Aaron, Al Geiberger, Dave Marr, Tom Kite and John Cook. I have to give a great deal of credit to these touring pros who came and gave support to Irwin in this event for the Children's Hospital.

I knew Jay Haas when he was playing junior golf in the St. Louis area. At that time, I was involved with managing the Greater St. Louis Junior Golf Program. Jay and his younger brother, who was in the pee-wee division, came from St. Clair Country Club in Belleville, Illinois, to participate. In 1972, my son, Tom, finished a distant second to Jay in a series of the St. Louis District junior club tournaments. There were junior events held each Friday over the course of the summer. There was never a question about Jay's future. I was in awe as I watched his short game. It was like observing a watch repairman handling the fine mechanism of a lady's watch. It brought to my mind watching Jerry West handle a basketball while he was playing at West Virginia University. Both Jay and Jerry were unique and stood out from the rest.

Hale Irwin's pro-am event started with a golf clinic emceed by Hale. Each of the touring professionals hit shots with their favorite club. When it came time for Leonard Thomson to demonstrate wood shots, he was restricted to a three wood in order to protect the homes beyond the practice range. One year, Evan "Big Cat" Williams was among the professionals. There was no way that they were going to turn him loose in a space restricted to about 275 yards. For his demonstration, the clinic adjourned to the first tee, a par four hole. When he hit his driver, he nearly drove the first green at Old Warson. His drive must have been nearly 350 yards. And that was when drivers had persimmon clubheads. That day I won the closest to the pin on a longish elevated par 3 hole by hitting a five wood, no less. My prize was a Ping putter presented by "Big Cat." A putter from the long drive champion.

Hale Irwin's tournament was usually played during May or early June. In 1977 the tournament was played during the early part of May. I was most fortunate that day to draw Al Geiberger as the pro for our group. It was just great to play with a golfer as capable and as pleasant as Al. I thought that I could move a golf ball pretty well, even though I was sixty-three years old at the time. When I did hit a pretty good drive, there was Geiberger's ball ahead of me by forty yards. About a month later, Geiberger shot 59 at the Danny Thomas Tournament in Memphis. That was great for me. I was able to tell anyone who would listen that this was a result of Al watching me play during the Hale Irwin pro-am.

About that time I was looking ahead to when I would retire, and I realized that it was merely four years away. I tried to think about what I would do with my time when I was no longer working. I considered the possibility of doing something with golf, of course. I thought that I might try teaching this game that I loved. After all, I had already been involved with teaching for nearly forty years. During the spring of 1977, I ran across an advertisement in Golf Digest magazine listing some of the golf schools that Golf Digest had scheduled for that year. One of them was a school for golfers with handicaps of six or less. Three of the teachers listed for that session were Bob Toski, Jim Flick and Peter Kostis. The fourth was Dick Murphy, who turned out to be the putting instructor. This school sounded interesting, and I thought it might provide me an insight into golf instruction.

Coincidentally, I had just read a series of articles by Jim Flick in *Golf World* magazine. He had written these articles while he was still in Cincinnati at Losantville Golf Club. In these articles, Flick broke down the golf swing into the finest detail and I was quite impressed. On the basis of all this, I decided to enroll in that five day school, which was held in southern Florida, at Boca West. The way it worked out, Bob Toski was just there for the last two or three days. Peter Kostis worked with the students on the line. He also lectured to us in the morning. I do not like to second-guess Peter, but at the time I thought the lectures he gave were over the head of the students who were not engineers or scientists and did not have Ph.D.s. He used golf shafts for his demonstrations of angle of attack, angle of incidence or angle of reflection. These are terms that only an engineer or physicist would comprehend. As a university teacher for forty years, I feel that I am qualified to say that it doesn't make sense to talk to a class unless you are certain that you are truly communicating with them.

Jim Flick handled the short game. When I spoke with Jim and told him that I had enjoyed the articles he had written for *Golf World*, he cut me short with, "We don't teach that anymore." So much for being impressed. I will say this for him: he could hit one-arm wedge shots better than anyone else I had ever seen, and he is a pleasant person. I do not believe that he should have been working under Toski. At the farewell dinner on Friday night, each member of the class was given photographs that were taken with the four instructors. These photos were then autographed by each of them. On mine, Jim Flick wrote, "Lee, please work on your setup." I wonder why he didn't tell that to me that earlier while the school was in session. Territorial rights?

On Saturday, before we left, arrangements had been made for the students from the class to play the golf course. After all the instruction we had, not one of us seemed to be able to hit the side of a barn, so to speak. However, after I got home, it didn't take me very long to get my game back and I did qualify for the USGA Senior amateur that was held that year at Salem Country Club's Donald Ross course, near Boston.

As a result of this experience at the Golf Digest school, I decided that if I were to give advice to a person who was interested in getting golf instruction, I would advise that person to find a teacher with a proven reputation and take weekly lessons for some period. This would avoid what I quoted from Henry Longhurst about "merely consolidating imperfections," which you will surely do if you work on your game without supervision. When a student takes music lessons, he or she takes these lessons on a regular schedule, usually weekly. At the end of each lesson, the student is given an assignment to practice before the next lesson. This is the way to avoid bad habits from setting in. I believe that what I am suggesting is not only best for effective golf instruction, but I am quite certain that it would cost considerably less than going to a five-day school such as the one I attended in 1977.

HISTORY AND DEVELOPMENT
OF THE GAME

Being an engineer, I have a great curiosity with regard to the origin and development of different things—almost everything. With golf having played such a large part in my life, over time I have delved deeply into the background of all aspects of the game. I am confident that anyone who reads this book will also have some interest in the highlights of the game and development of the tools that are used to play the game.

I consider the development in golf clubs to be very fascinating. A number of good books have been written on the history of golf. Many of these are large volumes. I do not intend to treat the subject in great detail. Those who have not been exposed to these publications will enjoy an abridged version, like this chapter.

THE BIRTH OF THE GENTLEMEN'S GAME

The game of golf is more than 500 years old. We know that in 1457 the Scottish Parliament ordained that golf "be utterly cryit doune and nocht usit." This drastic measure was taken because golf cut into the time that the citizens should have been practicing archery. In 1491, the Parliament passed another law much to the same effect. There must have been a change in the administration because by 1503 the King of Scotland was playing golf regularly. The earliest reference to golf being played at St. Andrews is dated 1552. The Royal and Ancient Golf Club was founded in 1754. However, that name was not officially bestowed upon it until 1834. The clubhouse that we see today was completed in 1854.

The British Open Championship was established in 1860, and

the first winner was Willie Park Sr. By 1867, the Patriarch of golf, Tom Morris Sr., had won the Open Championship for the fourth time. I have had a framed picture of "Old Tom" in my home for many years and I am looking at him now as this is being written. In 1870, Tom's son, Tom Morris Jr., won the Open Championship for the third time in succession and became owner of the belt. The tournament was not held in 1871, but in 1872 Tom Morris Jr. won it for the fourth time. It was about that time that his wife died, and a broken-hearted Tom Morris Jr. died just a few years later in 1875. His grave can be visited in St. Andrews. Between them, Tom Morris Sr. and Tom Morris Jr. won nine of the first thirteen British Opens. Willie Park Sr. won three of the other four. The first American to win the British Open was Jock Hutchinson in 1921. Other Americans soon followed. Walter Hagen won it in 1922 and 1924, Jim Barnes in 1925 and Bobby Jones, as an amateur, in 1926. Just before and after the turn of the century, the "Great Triumvirate," made up of Harry Vardon, James H. Taylor and James Braid, monopolized the British Open Tournament. Between the three of them, they won the tournament fifteen times.

GOLF COMES TO AMERICA

In this country, the U.S. Open and the U.S. Amateur tournaments were established in 1895. In 1904, Walter Travis won the British Amateur Championship using a center-shafted aluminum mallet putter. The Schenectady model putter he used is a valued asset in many antique golf club collections. In 1910, the British banned the use of center-shafted clubs (putters) considering that it had given Travis an unfair advantage. The ban on center-shafted putters was not lifted in Britain for many years. Travis was the first American to win the British Amateur. It wasn't until 1926 that another American, Jess Sweetster, won the British Amateur tournament. In 1913, Francis Ouimet, an amateur, beat Harry Vardon and Ted Ray by five strokes in a play-off for the U.S. Open Championship. Probably everyone reading this has seen the movie version of that historic event in The Greatest Game Ever Played. The Hollywood version of the play-off was changed to make the play-off seem much closer. Ouimet was no flash in the pan. He also won the U.S. Amateur the following year. In 1922, at the age of 20, Bobby Jones tied for the U.S. Open Championship with Gene Sarazen and H.L. Black and lost the playoff to Sarazen. During the following nine years, Jones, as an amateur, won four U.S. Opens, and was runner up four times. Jones won the British Open for the first time in 1926 and tied the scoring record set by James Braid in 1908. Jones was playing the difficult Royal Lytham and St. Anne's course when he tied the record. Braid set his record at Prestwick, which is no longer used as a British Open venue. During the qualifying rounds, Jones amazed the spectators by scoring 66 and 68, a total of 134 strokes for the two rounds. This was seven strokes better than his nearest rival.

To put things in their proper perspective, these low scores were made using wood-shafted golf clubs and under the rules of golf in effect at that time. For example, during that era and well into the time that I was playing competitive golf, a player was not permitted to clean his ball on the green. If the player was required to lift his ball, it had to be held in the same position as when it was when lifted and replaced so that it was exactly as it had been before it was lifted. Bobby Jones retired from competitive golf in 1930 at the age of 28. He is famous for winning the four tournaments that made up the Grand Slam in 1930, the year of his retirement. The four tournaments were the U.S. and British Opens and U.S. and British Amateurs.

Starting in 1931, Jones made a series of eighteen instructional films for Warner Brothers in Hollywood. The first twelve were entitled How I Play Golf, and the last six, How to Break 90. There was something of a problem in reaching an agreement about this series of films. Warner Brothers wanted the series entitled How to Play Golf. Jones insisted that there was more than one way to play golf, and Warner Brothers finally accepted his title, How I Play Golf. The movies were filmed at the Flintridge Country Club and Lakeside Golf Club in Los Angeles and included many Hollywood stars. The movie stars appearing in the instructional series of films included Joe E. Brown, Douglas Fairbanks, Jr., Edward G.

Robinson, Joan Blondell and Loretta Young. Among other things, it was amazing to see Jones playing so well from greenside bunkers using a niblic, the equivalent of a present-day nine iron. Jones, the amateur, was the first person to hold both the British Open and U.S. Open titles at the same time. I am forever grateful to Ely Callaway, the founder of Callaway Golf, for his gift of the two video tapes made from the Warner Brothers films. I continue to enjoy them today.

The development of the golf club makes a fascinating story. It could be a book by itself. Early golf clubs were fashioned from a single piece of wood. Some one-piece clubs were manufactured until the turn of the twentieth century. A.G. Spalding advertised their "One-Piece Clubs" in the late 1890s for the price of $2.00.

Naturally, most of the golf clubs made during the 19th century were made in Scotland. Among the famous club makers of woods at that time were Hugh Philp and the Forgans of St. Andrews, the McEwans, the Morris Family, the Dunns, the Patricks, and the Parks. These club makers mostly fashioned woods and putters. I was truly moved, on one occasion, when I was visiting the James River Country Club in Virginia. The club had a golf museum that contained a number of golf clubs made by Hugh Philp. Philp's clubs are so outstanding that I was as thrilled to see them as I would be to see a Ferrari or Lamborghini. What added to my wonder was that Philp was one of the earlier club makers. He died in 1856. Robert Forgan, his nephew, took over the business after Philp's death. The state of the art, before and during the 19th century, was such that the heads of the woods could not be drilled to accept the wood shaft. Instead, the club makers joined the head and shaft using what is known in carpentry as a scared joint. Both the hosel of the clubhead and the bottom of the shaft were beveled for an appreciable length after which glue was applied and whipping wound around the entire joint to add strength. These were referred to as scared-head clubs. Most of them were of the long nose variety. Many of these clubs had bone insert at the bottom to protect the head of the club against stones or other sharp objects on the golf course. Even putters were fashioned in the long nose style at that time.

The wood clubs had unusual names. The club that was used off the tee was referred to as a "Play Club." It was probably derived from the expression "play away." Other names for wood clubs included the spoon, short spoon, approach putter, baffy and cleek. There were rut or track irons, water rakes and water niblics made of steel. The word cleek was also applied to an iron similar to a one iron, as well as to a putter, which was known as a putting cleek. Many clubs of the middle and late 19th century had spooned faces. This referred to the concave curvature forged into the face of the clubhead. McEwan built a club called a grass driver. If the face was damaged on some of these old clubs, the repair was made using leather as a patch. During the time that the feather ball was in use, most of the golf clubs were woods. The reason for this was that the feather balls lasted much longer if they were not struck by iron clubs. About the only exceptions were the rut or track irons that were used to hit the ball out of wagon tracks. Some of the wooden putters of that era had brass faces. All of the irons made before 1900, during the guttie period, had smooth faces. Under dry conditions, and with a clean lie, a smooth-faced iron will impart as much backspin to the ball as an iron with grooves on the face.

RULE DEVELOPMENT

The rules of golf during the 19th century were not as forgiving as they are today. A player was seldom allowed to put his hand on the ball. While there weren't any paved golf car paths at that time, the courses did have equipment roads and many courses permitted wagons to cross the golf course. This was particularly true for the municipal golf courses. Wagon wheel ruts were common, as were equipment roads with loose gravel or cinders. Necessity being the mother of invention, the rut iron, or track iron, referred to above was created. The rule of the day was, "you hit it there, you play it from there." The only time you could lift your ball was when it interfered with a fellow competitor's ball on the green during a stroke play competition, and only if he asked you to lift it. In match play, a player did not lift his ball even if his ball was in the opponent's line of putt. This situation was referred to as a stymie, and the stymied player had to either go around or go over the opponent's ball. It was quite common to see a player use a niblic to play a stymie. Using a niblic to play a stymie doesn't do the green any good. If the player tried to use his niblic without taking a divot cut, he was not always successful. This rule lasted until 1951, the same year that the stroke and distance penalty for out of bounds was established.

When I was playing in match play competitions during the middle of the twentieth century, the rules were such that a player controlled his opponent's ball on the putting surface. If the player believed that an opponent's ball, near the hole, could be used to his advantage, he could require his opponent to leave the ball there while he putted or chipped. It was perfectly legal for him to carom his ball off the opponent's ball and into the hole. Of course, the rule has been changed since then. On a number of occasions when I was playing in competitions in the 1950s I had to play iron shots off of gravel equipment paths composed of limestone chips. These shots were hard on the soles of the iron clubs.

EARLY EQUIPMENT

Early golf courses did not begin to resemble the manicured courses that we expect to play on today. Consequently, putting cleeks used at that time had much more loft than the putters that are in use today. On some courses, a putt resembled a chip shot. In this country, on golf courses where it wasn't practical to bring water to the greens, the "green" surfaces were composed of sand treated with oil. A player was permitted to rake the line of the putt before putting.

Before the twentieth century, iron clubs were hand forged by metal workers. Some of the artisans that made early iron clubs were blacksmiths. These old irons were not produced in graduated sets as they are now. Clubs with more loft than the driving cleek were simply referred to as "lofters." Lofters were forged with various degrees of loft and not numbered.

A.G. Spalding and Bros. designed and sold many unusual clubs during the early twentieth century. Among them were a spring-faced iron, and the Cran Cleek. The Cran Cleek (1897) was an iron that had a hollow steel head with a wood insert. The wood insert didn't stand up very well when hitting the solid, hard gutta percha ball, which was in use at that time. However, it did take some of the shock out of the impact. The spring-faced club was declared illegal by the U.S.G.A. early in the century. It was this old ruling that was behind the controversy concerning golf clubs having a so-called "trampoline effect." Another innovation in irons during the 1920s was the "backspin club." These irons had wide, deep grooves. Among the manufacturers of backspin type clubs were Spalding, Wilson and Burke. One of Spalding's models of the backspin club had a waterfall pattern for the deep grooves on the face of the club. Spalding labeled these clubs as their "Dedstop" models. A change in rules did away with the backspin, or any deep groove irons during the early 1920s.

There was quite a fuss raised during the 1980s with regard to square grooves used on irons. The authorities claimed that square grooves imparted too much backspin and made iron play too easy. Some Ping irons I purchased in 1984 had these square grooves. I found evidence of their effectiveness by just looking at my golf ball. After several holes, the golf ball looked as if it needed a shave. This is easy to understand when we realize that the ball flattens on the face of the club and tries to climb up the face, due to the loft. As the ball flattens during impact, the soft cover penetrates the sharp grooves and tears up the paint.

Some other strange golf clubs appeared on the scene about 1925. These were giant niblics made in Scotland by Hendry & Bishop Ltd. and Cochrane Ltd. The heads were about four inches in diameter. Because of its large size, the head of the giant niblic was very thin in order to keep the weight at a reasonable value.

A particularly beautiful set of Chieftain woods was manufactured by MacGregor about 1928. The driver, brassie and spoon had fancy red, white and green inserts, and oval-shaped ivory back weights. This was about the prettiest of the "fancy face" clubs.

They were manufactured with both wood shafts and, later, with steel shafts. They sold for the exorbitant price of twenty-five dollars each. The top of the head had a diamond-shaped ivory insert that, in turn, had a black, green or red circular inlay to distinguish whether it was a driver, brassie or spoon.

During the early part of the twentieth century, there was no limit on the number of clubs that a player could have in his golf bag. As a result, some players carried as many as twenty-five golf clubs. Naturally, some of the clubs in the bag were not used during a round of golf. They were there "just in case." Later, when the number of clubs in the bag was limited to fourteen, it created problems for many players, even those who did not go overboard in the first place.

Many of the players liked to carry a one iron in their bag. By the time they had the complete set of irons through the wedge, plus a sand wedge and putter, there was only room for two woods. The first club to go was the brassie, or 2 wood, and most of the players carried only two woods, a driver and a three wood. At that time none of the players carried a five wood and only a few carried a four wood. The introduction of sixty and sixty-four degree wedges have made the choice of the fourteen clubs even more difficult. Tour players will alter their selection of clubs depending on the course to be played that week and/or the weather conditions. The average golfer finds a four and five wood easier to hit than a long iron. As a result, most sets of irons that are sold today contain 3–9 irons, plus a pitching wedge. A two iron is made available as a utility club. There has been a fairly recent trend to carry a seven wood and do away with the three iron. More than thirty years ago, I played with another golfer at a course at Biloxi, Mississippi, who had fourteen wood clubs in his bag. Even his putter was made of wood.

By the latter part of the 1920s, golf clubs began to be sold in "matched" sets. A complete set of woods included the driver, brassie and spoon. These were the equivalent of a set composed of a driver, 2 wood and 3 wood. The irons were a different matter; a standard set of irons was composed of a driving iron, mid iron, mid mashie, mashie iron, mashie, mashie niblic and niblic. The mashie niblic and niblic were sometimes "offset." In addition to the standard set, a player could also purchase a variety of utility clubs. Among these was the sky iron, a narrow-faced club that provided added elevation to a golf shot. Also available were chip mashies, pitchers, and sand "dabbers." The sand dabber had about the same loft as the niblic or pitcher, but a much wider face. Shortly after 1930, a spade mashie also came onto the scene. The loft on the spade mashie placed it between a mashie and a mashie niblic. This was during the period when there was no limit on the number of clubs the player could have in his or her golf bag.

Early in the 1930s, Burke marketed a jigger, or chipping club, which had a rounded bottom and identical lofted faces on both sides. The face had punch marks rather than lines. It could be used either right-or left-handed. The club was the same length as a putter. In addition, Burke offered the same head on a short shaft, which made the club length less than 18 inches. This club was called a "nub" iron. The short club was equipped with a standard size grip. The purpose of the club was to make it possible for a player to hit a ball from under a bush, or a low hanging evergreen tree, while he was in a kneeling position. The club could fit into a pocket of most golf bags.

It is amusing to examine the prices asked for new golf clubs and golf balls one hundred years ago. In 1897, The "Spalding" brand woods and iron clubs, their top line, were priced at $1.50 per club. The Cran Cleek, described earlier, was $2.00. Spalding also marketed a less expensive line of clubs, "Morristown," priced at $1.00 each. Morristown children's clubs were 75 cents each. Premium golf balls were $3.50 a dozen. These balls were still made of molded gutta percha at that time. A golfer could buy a golf ball press for $2.50, to be used for remolding gutta percha balls. Otherwise, the old balls could be sent to the factory for remolding at $1.00 a dozen.

All-leather caddy bags were priced at $4.00 to $5.00. If you wanted the bag to have a lock and a traveling cover, the price shot up to $7.50. It was guaranteed that this caddy bag would be accepted by railroads as baggage. Most golfing gloves were sold in pairs. The gloves were made of soft chamois, with open knuckles and perforated backs and palms. These were priced at $2.00 per pair. Fingerless gloves were priced at $1.00 per pair, or 50 cents for just the left hand glove.

By 1927, the price of golf clubs had "soared" to $15 each for the top line of "registered" woods, and about $8.00 each for irons. The term "registered" meant that a record was kept so that if a player broke or lost one of the clubs, an identical replacement could be obtained. By that time, some manufacturers offered a choice of either wood or steel shafts. In the 1927 Golf Guide, Spalding advertised the steel-shafted clubs as:

> Very popular with amateur and professional players; not affected by weather conditions; does not warp, rust or crack. Very good results to be had by beginners using the steel-shafted clubs.

The first golf club with a steel shaft actually appeared about 1916. The shaft had a hexagonal cross section, with perforated sides. This club was manufactured by Spalding under the Gold Medal label. It was called the Lard "Whistler," for the whistling sounds created by the perforations in the shaft as the club was swung. The club had deep groove scoring.

Steel shafts did not appear on the scene again until they were approved by the U.S.G.A. in 1926. They were first used for putters, but by 1930 they were being used for woods and irons, as well. There was considerable resistance from the public toward adopting the shiny steel shaft. Therefore, during the early 1930s, some steel shafts were painted to resemble the wood. In a few cases painted shafts were given a wood grain pattern. Further, the early steel shafts did not have the stepped configuration of most modern steel shafts. Many of them were made by wrapping sheet metal around a mandrel and welding the seam.

THE GOLF BALL

Any person interested in golf should be fascinated by the history of the golf ball and information as to why it behaves the way it does. Based on what we know, the game of golf dates back, at least, to the fifteenth century. There can be little doubt that the game that was played then does not resemble the modern game of golf. (See previous chapter, "The History and Development of the Game.")

THE FEATHERIE

While at first the game may have been played using a stone in place of a ball, the first known fabricated golf ball was the one that is referred to as the "featherie." This ball was made by stuffing a top hat full of wet feathers into a spherical leather pouch. Producing a golf ball in this manner was a long, tedious process. It is reported that a golf ball maker could produce only four "featheries" a day. The "featherie" made the game quite expensive and, therefore, limited the game of golf to a rather elite group. The first known price of a feathery, in 1452, was ten shillings, which would be the equivalent to close to ten dollars today. The featherie was used as the golf ball for several centuries. About 1850 a medical student at the University of St. Andrews, not being able to afford the price of the featherie, experimented with making a golf ball from a dry gum material that had been used as packing to protect a statue sent to his father. This material was gutta percha. Gutta percha is the milky juice or resin from the Isonandra Gutta tree, usually found in Malaya.

The story goes that the student softened the gum and then

molded it into the shape of a golf ball and baked it in an oven. On his first attempt to use it, the ball shattered after being struck a few times. After much experimenting, a new formula produced a more durable ball and the "guttie" established its place in the market. It was not only less expensive than the featherie, but it was more durable. The gutta percha ball soon replaced the featherie and was used for the next fifty years.

THE GUTTIE

The first gutties were made in a smooth mold. The ball did not stay in the air very long when hit with the play club, which was used as the driver at that time. After each round the golfers would have the guttie remolded to remove the nicks or cuts created by the iron clubs during a round. Some of the golfers did not remold the guttie and found that the nicked ball stayed in the air longer and went farther than the smooth ball. When this information got around, hammers were made with chiseled groves and the balls were "hand hammered" before being put into play. This led to making molds that produced markings on the golf ball during manufacture. Yet the solid gutta perch ball still had a problem of disintegrating after being in use for some time. The rules of golf covered such an occurrence. Rule 38, in effect at that time, read:

> If a ball split into separate pieces, another ball may be put down where the largest portion lies; or if two pieces are apparently of equal size, it may be put where either piece lies, at the option of the player. If a ball cracks or become unplayable, the player may change it on intimating to his opponent his intention to do so.[1]

DEVELOPMENT OF THE MODERN BALL

Just before the turn of the twentieth century, Coburn Haskell, an American, produced a wound rubber ball with a gutta percha cover. It was called a Bramble. This ball had pimples instead of dimples. The cover resembled the texture of a blackberry. The ball not only flew better it also putted better. In 1902, Laurie Auchterlonie won the U.S. Open using this new type of ball, setting a record by breaking 80 in all four rounds. The modern golf ball was born.

From then on it was just a matter of making one improvement after another, and this has never stopped. It would appear that some of the most recent "improvements" were really created for marketing purposes. There was a great deal of room for improvement at first and competition was the fuel for these improvements. The changes included both the cover and the inner construction. However, for many years the wound rubber ball was the standard. The manufacturers experimented with different cores for the ball. A list of the materials used for the core of a golf ball includes cork, gum, steel, celluloid, and several kinds of liquid centers. There was even one ball whose manufacturer claimed it contained radium for extra power. It was called the "Radio Ball." This was as ridiculous as recent balls that were purported to have titanium in them. Early twentieth century American and British golf balls had a diameter of 1.62 inches. About one-third of the way through the twentieth century, the USGA opted for a ball with a diameter of 1.68 inches. The Royal and Ancient Golf Society (R&A) continued with the 1.62 inch ball. At this time almost all golf balls had either mesh or dimple patterns and rubber had replaced gutta percha in the covers.

During World War II, the shortage of rubber almost did away with golf. George Worthington helped to produce golf balls from synthetic materials and kept the game alive. This eventually led to the surlyn cover, which became popular with higher handicap golfers because it was more difficult to cut through the cover with a topped iron shot. During the 1930s, Spalding manufactured the "Tournament" brand golf ball, "for greater distance." The cover was so soft and thin that a topped shot might actually peel off a part of the cover. It put a smile in the cover, to say the least.

Another variation that was introduced during the earlier part of the twentieth century was the "Floater" golf ball, when the USGA changed the weight to 1.55 ounces. This caused such an uproar that the ruling was rescinded the following year. This ball was the same size as the regular golf ball but was light enough to float.

Being a floater, it could be recovered from a water hazard. I found one some years ago in the water behind the 17th green at Bay Hill. On another occasion my wife and I played golf at "April Sound," a course not too far from Houston. At this course, instead of the usual driving range, we hit golf balls into the lake. The balls we hit were of the "floater" type. There was a floating net that helped to restrict the golf balls to a limited area in order to facilitate gathering them. The floater, being a lighter weight golf ball, did not go as far as a standard golf ball, which weighed 1.62 ounces.

The discussion to this point included the fact that a smooth guttie did not carry as far as a guttie with a nicked surface. It was also mentioned that in the process of development some golf balls were made with bramble patterns and this was followed by dimple and mesh patterns. Now we will look at why a golf ball does fly better with these cover patterns and whether there is an optimum pattern and depth of dimple. The reader will note that in the preceding sentence I used the term "fly." This was intentional because that is exactly what takes place.

ROTATION AND TRANSLATION

In aerodynamic theory, the lift of an object moving through air is defined by the equation: Lift = Air density times Velocity times Circulation. It is easy to envision the term "circulation" if you think that it resembles eddy flow or the rotational flow you see when water is draining from a sink. This is the equivalent to what creates the lift for an airplane wing due to the fact that the pressure above the wing is less than the pressure below the wing. When a golf ball is struck by a golf club that has loft, backspin is induced. As the ball flies it experiences both *rotation* and *translation*. The *rotation* is what we refer to as backspin, and the *translation* is the forward velocity of the golf ball. The effect of both the translation and the rotation cause lift forces to be applied to the golf ball. The dimples or any other cover pattern determine the amount of circulation and therefore lift that is experienced by the golf ball. We will examine each of these separately.

First we will look at translation. As a result of translation a force is developed that is referred to as air resistance or parasite drag, in aerodynamic terms. Assume that the ball is not spinning, but is moving through the air much the same as a knuckleball does in baseball. As the ball moves through air, the molecules of air on the surface move at the same velocity as the object. The molecules of air slightly above the surface do move, but not as fast as the ball. This process progresses until at some small distance from the surface of the ball the air is not affected by skin friction. The thickness of the air between the surface and the point where the air is not directly affected by the surface properties is called the boundary layer.

Boundary layer can occur in two forms. It can be laminar or turbulent. A laminar boundary layer is desirable for a streamlined object such as an airplane wing or fuselage. The reason for this is that for a streamlined object the major part of the drag is caused by skin friction and a laminar flow creates much less skin friction (drag) than does turbulent flow. However, for an object that is not streamlined, the major part of the air resistance is parasite drag, caused by the shape of the object. A spherical golf ball is considered to be a blunt object. Whether the air flow at the surface is laminar or turbulent makes a huge difference. The nature of a laminar flow boundary layer is such that it does not contain sufficient energy to adhere to the surface of the ball once it reaches the location of the largest dimension of the ball. Therefore, it separates from the surface and creates a large low pressure area, or wake, behind the sphere, which is even larger in area than the maximum projected area of the sphere. However, if we make the surface of the ball irregular or rough, the boundary layer becomes turbulent and the air flow will adhere to the surface of the ball well past the maximum diameter. As a result the low pressure area behind the ball is much smaller than it is under laminar flow conditions and far less parasite drag is created. Consequently, this will help to make the ball travel farther. A turbulent boundary layer was created when the guttie developed nicks.

Now let us examine this matter of rotation and the resulting circulation. From the equation that was presented earlier, it is clear that the amount of lift is directly proportional to the circulation. Lift is the major force that keeps a ball struck by a driver, which doesn't have much loft, in the air. If the ball surface is perfectly smooth, the backspin will not affect the air around it sufficiently to create a satisfactory amount of circulation. The markings on the cover provide the necessary conditions required to produce more circulation (lift), which means added distance. In summary, the marking on the golf ball both reduces the drag and increases the lift, a win-win situation.

This brings us to the subject of what the best cover pattern is to produce optimum distance. There is no one pattern that is best for all golfers. A touring professional will prefer a cover pattern that produces less lift than the pattern that might be best for a higher handicap man or woman who does not spin the ball as much. If there is too much lift, a ball hit by a touring professional will climb too high and the golf ball's energy will be wasted on elevation rather than distance. When Acushnet, the makers of the Titleist golf ball, first changed from the old symmetrical dimple pattern, their ball created too much lift for better golfers and too much distance was lost due to elevation. The company then produced two other covers, which had the same marking but less depth. These were called Pro Trajectory and Low Trajectory. It appears that this led other golf ball manufacturers to change their cover patterns and all sorts of geometric patterns appeared on the scene. I doubt that these fancy patterns did much to improve the performance of the basic golf ball. With regard to the depth of the markings, there is a certain range of depths that is useful. If the markings are deeper that about 0.010 inches, the amount of circulation will not be increased much but the drag will increase, and the result will be inferior.

I had an amusing experience some years ago that demonstrated what has been described above. One summer I visited a golfing friend of mine who was vacationing with his wife on the Connecticut shore. Naturally, I had my golf clubs with me. Bob and I had an interesting round of golf on a twelve-hole golf course. This by itself was a new experience to me. We played the last six holes twice, but from different tees. That evening, along with our wives, we dined at a restaurant that was located right on the beach. Since it was early summer the days were long and it was still light when we finished dinner. As we left the restaurant we noticed that there was a driving range on the beach near the restaurant. The range was equipped with mats for the teeing area and the golf balls were hit toward targets anchored in the in the sand. After a fine dinner preceded by several drinks my friend and I naturally decided to display our golf prowess to our wives.

Both Bob and I were low handicap golfers at that time. When I hit a good drive I could normally get about 270 yards. Bob and I got our drivers and proceeded to demonstrate our skills, with me being the first to hit. I felt as if I had hit the first ball pretty well on the center of the club face. The ball stayed low and carried about 80–90 yards. I tried several more with the same result. After Bob finished laughing he went at it. His best efforts were also in the 80–90 yard range. By now I was both sober and confused. I examined the golf balls that remained in the bucket and found that they not only had no dimples but were as smooth as glass. Evidently, as the balls were constantly hit into the abrasive sand, the paint was removed. Whenever this occurred the balls were repainted. After a few cycles of this process, the dimples became completely filled with paint and the surface of the entire cover became uniformly slick. This affected the boundary layer and therefore the circulation adversely, and the ball just couldn't "fly."

THE GOLF COLLECTORS SOCIETY AND ADVENTURES IN EUROPE

In 1965 the U.S. Open was played at the new Bellerive Golf Course near St. Louis, Missouri. By this time live golf was aired on television. The state of the art at that time limited the live telecasts to the last four holes. There was a tower behind each of the last four greens. The new Bellerive course had Bermuda grass fairways when it was first built. At the time that the tournament was to be played, in June, the Bermuda grass had not yet fully changed its color from dormant yellow to green. In order to look better on the TV screen the fairways of the last four holes were sprayed with green paint.

I had moved to St. Louis in 1963 to accept the position as Dean of Engineering at St. Louis University. By this time I had become interested in other aspects of golf, which included collecting golf-related items. There are a number of different categories available to collectors. I started with wood-shafted golf clubs (antiques), golf books and golf art. During the spring of 1971, I ran across an advertisement that offered some old golf clubs for sale by someone in Pennsylvania. I responded to this ad and as a result I was able to purchase some old hand-made scared-head woods dating back to the late nineteenth century. Evidently, as a result of this purchase, I was contacted by another man from the Philadelphia area, Joe Murdoch, who was also a golf collector. Joe wrote that he was going to be in St. Louis for the Ryder Cup matches, which were to be held that fall in St. Louis at Old Warson Country Club. He suggested that we meet during this time. I replied, telling him that

I would be there for the entire week of the matches since I was one of the sponsors for the Ryder Cup Matches.

During our meeting he told me that he and another man from Akron, Ohio, Bob Kuntz, were in the process of forming a golf collector's society, and asked if I would I be interested in joining them. What a question! I went further, and suggested that the new organization might schedule an annual meeting, which would contain show-and-tell sessions as well as programs on how to restore antique clubs. Bob Kuntz was the expert on antique golf club restoration. As a result, the Golf Collectors Society was born, and I was one of the founding members. The Society now has over 4000 members worldwide who collect a total of forty-three different types of golf-related items. The classifications include golf pencils, logo tees, toys, ball markers, signature balls and on and on. By now, the Golf Collector's Society has a great many commercial members and is no longer the simple show-and tell society of the early 1970s. In the 1970s, good sources for antique golf clubs included the Goodwill and Salvation Army retail stores, where one could find barrels with wood-shafted clubs for prices ranging from ninety-five cents to five dollars. Over the years that I was actively collecting golf material, my collection grew to include 550 antique golf clubs, 300 golf books, 150 classic golf clubs and a few dozen pieces of golf art. For a time I had all of these on display in my home. Sadly, I had to part with most of my collection later, when I retired and no longer had room for my collection.

When I reached the semi-ripe age of fifty five, I became active in senior golf. For several years, I enjoyed playing in tournaments as a member of the Western Senior Golf Association. During 1977, I qualified for the USGA Senior Amateur Tournament, which was played at Salem Country Club in Salem, Massachusetts, on their fine Donald Ross designed golf course.

During the late 1960s and 1970s, as part of my work, I attended the Paris Air Show, which is held every other year. This entailed spending a week in Paris each time. On each occasion I arranged to combine this with my vacation time and spend a total of three weeks overseas. Either before or after the week of the Paris Air

Show, I spent two weeks driving around Europe playing golf in different countries. I played in Denmark, Germany, Belgium, France, Portugal, England, and of course Scotland. I drove through all these countries with their different languages and never experienced a bad moment. I will be forever grateful to Paris because it was there that I was introduced to escargot. After I returned from my first trip to Paris I continued to eat escargot at every opportunity until my physician became concerned with my cholesterol numbers.

On my second bi-annual trip to Europe, in 1969, I took my wife and son, Tom, with me. We started our golf tour at Turnberry, not far from Glasgow and Troon. This was my first experience driving a car on the left side of the road from a right side seat. The first time I saw a car coming at me on the wrong side of the road I felt like climbing a utility pole. However, it didn't take long to adjust. In fact when I returned to the United States, I found myself looking in the wrong direction for traffic when I had to cross a street.

When we were there the Turnberry golf courses were reserved for two ball matches until 9:00 a.m. These could be either singles matches between two players or foursome matches with four players playing two balls. I thought this was a great idea. It made it possible to play 18 holes of golf in two hours. I knew that this would never be accepted over here because, for one thing, at clubs in the U.S. everyone is required to post 18-hole scores in order to maintain their handicap. Also, I can't imagine many of the club members over here being willing to give up the early morning hours on the course for these two ball matches. Most American's never see foursomes playing two ball matches except during the Ryder Cup and President's Cup matches.

The 1969 trip was my first experience on a Scottish golf course, which did not have watered fairways. Evidently, 1969 was a very unusual year, as the weather was warm, dry and practically without wind. We played at Turnberry in short-sleeved shirts; it was that balmy.

On the first hole of the Ailsa course I hit quite a good drive.

When we reached my ball I estimated that I had 165 to 170 yards to the green. I reached over to my golf bag and started to extract a five iron. My 70-year-old caddie put his hand over mine and said, "Nae, laddie, take a nine iron."

I looked at him as if he was out of his mind. I said, "It looks to me as if it is 165 to 170 yards."

His reply was, "Aye, it's exactly that, but I seen y' hit your drive. Hit a nine." I took the nine iron and hit it well. Sure enough it landed well short of the green. But the ball then proceeded to bounce and roll onto the green pin high. Welcome to golf in Scotland.

We had the same nice weather at our next stop, which was Gleneagles. Then we went on to St. Andrews, arriving there on a Sunday. The weather when we arrived was unchanged; it was beautiful. Since the Old Course was closed on Sunday, we walked the course and looked forward to our early tee time the following morning. Our room at the Old Course Hotel overlooked the double green for the 2nd and 16th holes. When we looked outside the next morning we got some idea of what we were in for. Overnight the weather had changed from one of the nicest days to the worst weather I have ever experienced on a golf course. If this had been anything other than the Old Course I would never have ventured out. This was the Scotland I had read about. My son and I got into our rain gear and started out with our caddies. The rain and wind were so fierce that I had to take off my glasses and depend on the caddy to follow the ball. I shot an even 80 and was very proud of that considering the conditions. On the Old Course we ran into something I had never seen before on any golf course. The seventh and eleventh holes cross each other. There was a sign on the seventh fairway that read, "Homeward bound players have the right of way." When we got back to the hotel we were directed to a "drying room." There was special room on the lower level that had benches made with slotted seats to allow the air to circulate through and help to dry our outer clothes and equipment. This was another first for me. We played Carnoustie the next day. It was still cold and windy, but at least it was dry.

A few years later I had a wonderful experience in Denmark. I had flown directly to Copenhagen from New York on Pan Am, finally arriving at my hotel during the afternoon. First thing the following morning, I called the Rungsted Golf Club and spoke with the secretary. I told him that I was visiting from the U.S. and would like to play their course, if it was possible. The secretary hemmed and hawed and finally asked me when I wanted to play. I told him that because of my schedule it would have to be that afternoon. More silence followed and finally he told me that, yes, it would be possible. Then he asked me what my handicap was. This threw me for a loop. All I wanted to do was play their course and now he wanted to know about my handicap? By this time my handicap was up to six and I told him that. After another long silence he told me that I should be there ready to play at 1:00 p.m.

I arrived at Rungsted and proceeded to the practice putting green. Just before one o'clock I went to the clubhouse to let them know that I was there. I was then told that I would be playing with three other men. In the few hours since I had talked to the secretary he had rounded up three players to join me. The highest handicap among the three was seven. All three spoke perfect English. One was the Ping distributor for the Scandinavian countries, one was a doctor and the third was a local businessman. I had an absolutely wonderful day. After the game we drank Tuborg beer and swapped lies for a couple of hours. I consider this to be the finest display of hospitality that I have ever experienced.

A very humorous incident occurred in the aforementioned 1969 trip that put me in the national spotlight for a brief moment. At that time, Tom, 13, was not enthusiastic about the idea of giving up three weeks of his summer vacation to travel in Europe. As a form of inducement, I came up with an idea. I suggested that he could collect sand from a bunker of each golf course that we played and start a collection. Tom liked that and surprised me by actually becoming enthusiastic. I bought a dozen glass vials in which to collect the sand. Almost the first thing we did each time played a new course was to have Tom fill an empty vial with sand and label it. We collected eleven vials during the trip. On our flight back these vials were packed in the suitcase that held our soiled laundry in order to protect them.

Having come on a nonstop flight from London to Chicago, we had to go through customs at O'Hare airport. The customs people usually opened one bag and that was that. As luck would have it, they opened the bag that contained the laundry and found the vials filled with sand. The customs official asked what was in the eleven vials. When I told him that the vials contained sand from the golf courses we had played, he gave me a queer look. He then informed me that I was not allowed to bring foreign soil into the country for fear of contamination. Well, here we had gone to all this trouble and now the sand was being confiscated. Also, here was my thirteen-year-old son seeing his father being pushed around. I protested vigorously and said to the customs official, "Now look here. We have brought this collection over four thousand miles. We aren't about to lose it. You can take the sand now, if you must, but I want it returned." With that I gave him a card with my name and address. I felt that we would never see the sand again.

The following day the *Chicago Daily News* carried a feature story on the first page of Section B of the newspaper about this strange university dean who collects sand from golf courses all over the world. My sister called to tell me about it and then mailed a copy of the article to me. That did not end it. The wire services picked up the story and it was distributed all over the country and who knows where else. People sent me clippings, which had been used as fillers in some cases, from large important publications such as the *Mississippi Press* in Pascagoula, Mississippi, and the *Eagle* in Cheyenne, Wyoming.

When the *Post Dispatch* in St. Louis picked this up, they dispatched their sports reporter, Bill Beck, and a photographer to our home. The paper ran a fairly extensive article accompanied by large picture of Tom and me. Shortly before this interview, lo and behold, I received a package in the mail from the customs office, with the eleven vials of sand. It appeared that one of the vials had been open and some of the sand removed for assay. I nearly went into hysterics. The photo in the *Post Dispatch* included Tom and me and the eleven vials of sand.

In subsequent years each time I went to the Paris Air Show I took my golf clubs with me and when I played golf at new courses, I continued to collect sand to add to the collection. I added sand from Denmark, Germany, Belgium, France, Portugal and some of the islands in the Caribbean and Hawaii. Later I picked up a rack with nice screw-cap glass containers, transferred the contents to the new vials and labeled each container of sand with the course of origin. This collection is now on display in Tom's office in San Antonio.

I noticed one marked difference between most European golf courses and those in the United States. Most of the American courses I have played have cut fairways directly in front of the tees or light rough with a mowed path leading to the cut fairway. If there is rough in front of the tee, the rough is not very deep because if it was it would slow up the game. A golfer can top his tee shot and still have the ball roll a considerable distance. Most of the golf courses that I played in Europe posed severe problems for the golfer for a considerable distance directly in front of the tees. This appeared in the form of very tall grass at Turnberry, or rough terrain and rocks like that I found at the Club de Golf de Estoril at Cascais near Lisbon. I could only gather that the European golfers, particularly women, took more lessons and learned to get the ball into the air every time. Many of the female American country club golfers I had seen would not be happy on European golf courses. A few of the parkland golf courses that I did visit in Scotland were more forgiving.

On one of my European junkets, I played the St. Cloud golf course near Paris. I was given the courtesy of playing the course but not much more than that. I was assigned a female caddy who put my clubs on a pull cart. She spoke only French and as a result we didn't communicate much. It was a warm day in June and my caddy wore a wool pants suit. It didn't take long for me to decide that it worked better if I stayed upwind of the caddy with her cart.

On the back nine I saw a strange sight in the right rough that I did not understand. There was a deep excavation about fifty to sixty feet long and nearly half that wide. I tried to ask my French caddie what it was. By using some fractured French and hand gestures, and after my caddie said something about "les avion and les boche," I gathered that during the World War II a German airplane was shot down and crashed there. Rather than fill it in, the wreckage was removed and the excavation was seeded with grass. This was a first for me.

As you can see, when I say that golf has been an important part of my life, it may be an understatement.

CONSULTING FOR THE GOLF INDUSTRY

I retired from my position as Dean of Engineering at St. Louis University in 1981 and moved to the San Diego area, where there would be an opportunity to play golf at least twelve months a year. That certainly turned out to be a good choice.

In San Diego, I first started to play golf at Lomas Santa Fe Country Club, which is located in Solana Beach. It was a nice layout with narrow fairways. This suited my game perfectly. This was the course on which I first shot my age, after coming close several times. When I was 71 years old I finally shot 70. Since I was one under par going into the last few holes, I didn't feel any pressure toward the end of the round. As I added a few more years it became increasingly easier to shoot my age until finally I did it almost every time I went out. I didn't have any trouble keeping my swing together. One of the things that helped was that I had always enjoyed practicing as much as playing. It certainly did pay off in results and provided enjoyment at the same time.

THE CALLAWAY PATENT

A year or so after I arrived on the west coast I received a telephone call from someone who introduced himself as Richard Parente. He told me that he was associated with two other people and they had formed a new golf club company. He went on to tell me that they were faced with a patent problem. He wanted to know if I would be willing to sign on as a consultant and help them with their problem. He went on to say that they had gone to the engineering departments at one or more of the universities in the area seeking help without any success. When they were meeting with some of the staff at San Diego State University, one of the engineering faculty members told them that he knew a member at his country club that he felt might be able to help them. The person he referred to was me. This professor was a member of my club with whom I had played golf several times.

When Parente described their problem I told him that it sounded interesting to me but I would need to know more about it. I agreed to visit their facility, which at that time was located at Cathedral City, near Palm Springs. When I went there I met the other two principals, Dick de La Cruz and Ely Callaway. Ely Callaway had recently sold his winery and was now involved in a different type of business venture.

The name of the new company was Callaway Hickory Stick Co. They were planning to manufacture a golf club that would have a hickory shaft with a steel tube as its central core. At first they planned to limit their production to putters and wedges. The hickory shafts were drilled using a rifle barrel drill, which could bore three shafts at a time. Ely Callaway had included arrangements to market signature putters signed by Paul Runyan and Billy Casper.

The problem that confronted them was that the United States Patent Office had rejected their patent application on the basis of a conflict. Evidently the patent office considered that the golf club in the Callaway patent application to be similar to another golf club for which a patent had been issued about fifty years earlier. Since the conflicting patent was old, it was now in the public domain. Even so, the old patent was an obstacle to the Callaway patent application. Ely Callaway was a shrewd business man, certainly one of the shrewdest I ever had the pleasure of meeting and working with. The patent was important to him because he was looking ahead to the foreign market as well as the domestic market. He knew that he would not be able to sell his clubs overseas, in Japan particularly, unless the club held a United States patent. The problem sounded interesting and I agreed to try to help them. There went my retirement!

The golf club of the older patent also had a hickory shaft.

However, instead of a steel tube it had a tapered steel rod as its core. The tapered steel rod extended down from the butt end of the shaft to a point near the clubhead. The clubhead was fastened to the hickory shaft by a rivet, much the same as the other irons of that era. By contrast, the clubhead of the Callaway model was attached to the hollow steel tube rather than the wood part of the shaft.

I looked into the patent of the earlier club and could not find that it had ever been built and marketed. It was readily apparent to me as to why it might not have been put into production. However, proving to the United States Patent Office that the older patent and the new Callaway club were different from each other was another matter. The Patent Office not only uses prior art for their criteria, but also whether the new patent application could be classified as "obvious," something that could be seen as the next logical step in development.

I set about analyzing the club with the tapered steel rod. In the first place it would be next to impossible to produce the golf club shown in the old patent at a reasonable price. However, this is not a valid argument to use with the patent office. The patent office does not care whether the idea in the patent is practical, only that it is not like any earlier patent either here in the United States or elsewhere in the world.

I calculated the weight of the tapered steel rod as shown in the old patent drawings. This solid rod would be so heavy that there was very little weight left available for the clubhead if the total weight were to fall within reasonable values. It was clear that because of the heavy tapered rod, the club would not only have little feel but it would not be able to hit a golf ball an acceptable distance. I decided to design mathematical models for both golf club designs and then to calculate the performance of each club based on the known features from the patents. The calculations proved my assumption to be correct. We then tested the Callaway club using a golf ball driving machine. The test results agreed with my mathematical analysis of the Callaway club within two percent. This was well within acceptable limits of experimental error.

The model analysis was sufficient proof that the golf club of the older patent was a golf club in appearance only. This proof was accepted by the patent office, Callaway was issued a patent and Callaway Hickory Stick Co. was now in business. Ely Callaway was delighted and I was asked to stay on as a consultant.

Not much later Callaway decided to expand the line to include a full set of irons. Ely Callaway was a distant relative of the Bobby Jones family. He was able to make arrangements with the Jones family to use the Bobby Jones' signature on the line of new irons. I had a vintage 1931 Bobby Jones wood in my antique golf collection with the Bobby Jones signature on the crown. This was different from the set marketed by Spalding in the 1930s that carried the Robt. T. Jones, Jr. signature. Callaway wanted to copy the signature on my club for his new clubs. It is my understanding that Jones never did like the name "Bobby." Ely Callaway contracted with Neiman Marcus to carry the Callaway line and have the clubs included in the Neiman Marcus catalog. The price of Callaway clubs was always on the high end. Ely demanded quality and he priced his clubs accordingly. He used the theory that if the price was high the product would be judged to be superior. It not only worked, it worked very well.

Because of the weight of the heavy steel-lined hickory shafts, the clubs were not nearly as playable as golf clubs made with steel shafts. Further, by this time graphite shafts had appeared on the scene and were being accepted in a big way. The graphite shafts could be half the weight of steel shafts and less than one-third the weight of the Callaway steel-lined hickory shafts.

After a year or so, Ely Callaway brought Richard C. Helmstetter into the organization. Helmstetter had been in billiard cue manufacturing in Japan. He invested in the Callaway company and with his first-hand knowledge of Japanese marketing became a valuable asset. He was given the title of vice president. Evidently, the new arrangement was not to the liking of Parente and De La Cruz and they left the Callaway organization. By this time the name of the company had been changed from Callaway Hickory Stick Co. to Callaway Golf and the company had moved to

Carlsbad, a suburb north of San Diego. This was when Callaway Golf started to develop the Big Bertha metal woods. The name Big Bertha was Ely Callaway's idea. The first time I heard about the name was when we were on our way to Los Angeles with Paul Runyan, who had an interest in the company, to visit a patent attorney. Ely Callaway proposed the name of the long range World War I German artillery piece. He picked a winner!

As I mentioned earlier, Ely Callaway was a very shrewd business man. Not surprisingly, he was not knowledgeable about either the technical aspects of golf ball and golf club physics or the manufacturing process. Perhaps because he was a pretty fair golfer, he felt that he knew more than he actually did. Callaway's mind was always active. Every once in a while he would come up with an idea that was not at all practical. On these occasions I would tell him, "Ely, this will not work because it violates the laws of physics, and you can't argue with physics." Evidently, he heard that remark often enough so that he remembered it. Later, for some time, the expression "you can't argue with physics" was included in Callaway Golf Co. advertising.

At the outset, since the business was just starting up, I only charged Callaway fifty dollars an hour for my services as a consultant. It amused me, during this early period, when some of our sessions ran more than a couple of hours, Ely Callaway would ask me if the "meter was still running."

The next major step was the Callaway line of S2H2 irons with the "unique" drilled through hosel. At this stage the company really took off and success was assured. The drilled through hosel of S2H2 irons was not really a new idea. In my antique golf club collection I had a wood-shafted iron that was made in Scotland, circa 1905, and in which the hickory shaft also penetrated the steel head. Wilson also built steel-shafted irons during the 50s or 60s that included this feature.

SHIFTING WEIGHTS

A short time after they left Callaway Golf I was, again, contacted by Richard Parente and Dick De La Cruz. They informed me that they were now involved in a new project with a man from the Rancho Santa Fe area, also near San Diego. The project involved what they considered to be a new concept in golf clubs. The new idea was to build woods and irons with adjustable weight ports, which permitted a golfer to vary both the total weight as well as the weight distribution of the club. At this point in time, swing-weight was a popular topic in the golf world. The new company was to be known as Players Golf. Dick De La Cruz was the golf club designer. It was his job to convert the concept into a market-able golf club. Of course, the new group also wanted to obtain a patent for the Players golf clubs. That is why I was contacted. Again, there was a problem with the patent office with regard to "prior art."

The new Players clubs were designed to incorporate threaded sockets that would accept weight plugs. The plugs were com-posed of materials that had different densities. By employing a trial and error method, the combination that would best suit the individual could be found. The Rules of Golf permit a player to alter the characteristics of a club between rounds but not during a single round of golf. This feature made it possible for a golfer to fine tune the golf clubs after he had purchased them. There were three-threaded sockets at the back of each iron and three smaller weight sockets around the perimeter of the woods. The putter was equipped with two sockets for interchangeable weights. Each set of golf clubs was supplied with an assortment of weights made of aluminum, brass and tungsten. Brass weighs nearly the same as the stainless steel body of the iron and putter. Aluminum weighs about one-third (1/3) as much as stainless steel. And tungsten weighs about 2.4 times as much as stainless steel. This variation provided a considerable amount of flexibility for altering the char-acteristics of the golf clubs, including the putter. By varying the heel and toe weights in the longer irons, many golfers were able to improve their long iron accuracy. A golfer would also be able to change the weight of his or her putter in order to adapt the putter to the speed of the greens at different courses.

I came up with an original idea for the design of a swingweight balance that could be produced at a cost that was small enough so that the balance could be included free with each set of clubs. My swingweight balance would be composed mostly of plastic with a counterbalance made of metal. The balance contained circular holes or depressions to accommodate a standard golf ball. The golf ball was the substitute for the slide usually found on a swingweight balance. The holes or depressions were spaced strategically so that moving the golf ball one space would represent a change of one swingweight point. The balance covered swingweight values from C-0 to E-0, the entire range normally used for both men's and women's golf clubs.

As mentioned earlier, the Players golf clubs conformed to the rules of the United States Golf Association. Unfortunately, the company failed due to insufficient funding for advertising and other promotions. As I write this in 2006, the use of variable weights has surfaced again. TaylorMade's newest driver, and some of their fairway clubs, employ a variable weighting system.

Like most drivers and fairway woods sold today, the new TaylorMade clubs are made of titanium, which is stronger than stainless steel, yet weighs just a little more than half as much. As a result of using lightweight titanium for the shell of the golf club it is possible to distribute a considerable amount of the weight of the clubhead to strategic locations, which alter the performance of the golf club. The moveable weights can be concentrated at the toe or heel or both. They can also be located at the back of the head in order to move the center of gravity farther back. If the supplemental weighting is located near the perimeter of the clubhead, it will increase the polar moment of inertia of the clubhead and thereby help with resisting rotation that results from off-center impacts. As the center of gravity is moved back it increases the amount of gear effect and this can also be useful for off-center contacts with the golf ball. When Players Golf came up with this concept they applied it to a solid wood clubhead, and therefore didn't have as much flexibility. Recently, I have observed that many of the touring professionals are using putters with configurations that place much of the weight considerably behind the putter face.

On off-center contacts these putters will probably produce some gear effect that can compensate for off-center impact error as well. Since the face of the putter is flat, rather than curved as it is on a driver, the correction may be significant. The amount of correction will vary with the distance that the center of gravity of the putter is behind the face of the putter.

The advent of graphite shafts was the first major change in golf clubs since the steel shaft was made legal and introduced in 1926. During all the years that golf clubs were equipped with steel shafts, manufacturers of golf clubs have used the swingweight balance system to match golf clubs in a set. Until the advent of the graphite shaft, most drivers were 43 inches long and the clubs varied one half inch in length between numbers. Most manufacturers made irons with the five iron having a length of 37 inches. The average male golfer was fitted with golf clubs that were in the swingweight range of D-0 and D-2. Ladies golf clubs were one-half inch shorter. This placed the ladies clubs in the swingweight "C" range. I believe that some manufacturers used the same clubheads for men's and ladies irons because the half inch difference in length reduced the swingweight about five or six points and put it into the "C" range. Consequently most women used clubs that were too heavy for them.

Most steel shafts weigh a little over four ounces. If the same clubhead was fitted with a graphite shaft that weighs only two ounces, the swingweight drops well into the C range. For no good reason this is not considered to be acceptable. As long as the weight of the clubhead and the clubhead speed remained the same, the golf ball will fly just as far. But, because the lighter shaft put the club in the swingweight range normally used for women's clubs, it was believed that the public would think it was a weaker club. Therefore, in order to bring the clubs back into the "men's range," men's clubs with graphite shafts are made one-half inch longer and clubhead weights were also adjusted, if necessary.

I disapprove of the practice employed by some club manufacturers and golf club repairmen when trying to match clubs in a set. If the swingweight of a finished club does not match the desired value, the difference is corrected by methods that often affect the integrity of the golf club. If the swingweight is too great, lead tape is used under the grip. This reduces the swingweight even though it increases the total weight. It does nothing for the clubhead. To make matters worse, a golfer loses some club feel with that club. If the swingweight of the finished club is too low, lead shot is added inside the hosel and tamped down with some epoxy to keep it from rattling. Here, again, the added weight does not go into the hitting part of the clubhead and that club will not deliver the performance that it should. A more detailed discussion on the subject of swingweight is treated later in this book.

One of the companies that I worked with as a consultant had a designer who came up with the idea for an ultra lightweight golf club. This was achieved, primarily, by using an ultra-light shaft and a very lightweight grip. Instead of the usual 50 gram grip these clubs had a thin wrap around type grip weighing less than 20 grams. Special graphite shafts with oversize butt diameters were required so that the completed golf club could have normal grip dimensions. In order to have the completed club fall into the D-0 to D-2 swingweight range, the clubheads had to be made lighter. Between the lighter grip and the lighter clubhead, the completed driver weighed approximately eleven ounces. I was more than a little surprised that the people who made the decision to manufacture this new golf club did so without asking my opinion when it was in the planning stage. I would have certainly discouraged them because there wasn't any rationale to support the concept. The first I heard of it is when they told me that "we are betting the farm on this one." They lost the farm.

When they removed thirty grams from the weight of the grip the swingweight increased by about six points. This then made it necessary to remove weight from the head to bring the swingweight of the golf club to the D-0 to D-2 range. If they had been considering the more meaningful term, moment of inertia, it would have revealed that changing to the lighter grip would not have made a measurable difference to the moment of inertia. The reason being that the grip of the club is under the hands of the person swinging the club. This is just another case where employing swingweight can lead you down the wrong path.

I am quite certain that the ultra lightweight club was tested on a golf club testing machine. The results from the tests would be pretty good, although they must have lost some distance because of the lighter weight clubhead. I doubt that a player would swing this lighter club any faster than he would a 13-ounce club because it had a lighter clubhead.

The reaction of most golfers to this configuration was negative. Man, being a creature of habit, would need to make a conscious effort to adjust to a change of fifteen percent in total weight of the club. The fact that the swingweight was the same as the golfer's former club did not mean that the feel was the same. It was not! Swingweight is a measure taken about a fulcrum that is fourteen inches from the butt end of the golf club. A right handed golfer gets the feel of the club with his left hand since it is the left arm that is straight at address and throughout most of the swing. I tried the club and because of all the years I played with a heavier club I did not like the feel. The folly of this golf project could have been predicted, but no one asked.

GOLF SWING FUNDAMENTALS

It is my opinion that a person cannot play golf to his or her full potential unless certain fundamentals are followed, and I do mean *all* of these fundamentals. This will be easier for beginners to do than for players who have been playing with bad habits for some time. Habits are difficult to break. However, it can be done with practice and patience. It depends on your mind set. The rewards make it worth while. You cannot wish yourself into a good golf swing.

In my own case I did not have the opportunity to play or practice much until I was thirty-five years old. The depression, seven years of university education, World War II and the GI Bill of Rights prevented me from putting in as much time as I would have liked. Fortunately, I was not saddled with a bunch of bad habits to overcome. As a result, when I did finally have the time to put into my golf game, it went together quite rapidly and my handicap went down to scratch in only two seasons.

THE FOUNDATION

Just as a building must have a good foundation, it is just as important for the golf swing to have a good foundation. In golf we also start from the ground, which provides the anchor for the feet, and work up from there. If the feet are too close together it is difficult to keep your balance during a full swing. If the stance is too wide, it is difficult to coordinate the legs with the upper parts of the body. The distance between a golfer's feet at address should be much like that used by a tennis player waiting to return a serve or a basketball player who is ready to go in whatever direction is called for. In other words, you want to have an athletic stance. Somewhere about shoulder width is about right for the full swing. Slight adjustments can be made later after you are comfortable with what you are doing and when you are called on to compensate for the particular golf shot with which you are faced.

The placement of the feet should be such that it helps to accomplish your objective. In this case I recommend a golf swing in which the hip turn is restricted on the back swing, and encouraged as you are clearing your hips on the downswing. I have always preferred a stance where, for a right-handed golfer, the right foot is perpendicular to the line of flight. This aids in restricting the hip turn on the backswing. The left foot is turned out slightly toward the target. This helps the hips on the downswing. The toes of your shoes should be parallel to the intended line of flight. The shoulders should also be parallel to the line of flight at address.

Working up from the feet, the knees should be slightly bent so that you are in a partial sitting position. If the legs are straight and the knees locked, it is impossible to make an athletic swing. Do not overdo this slight sitting position. You just want your knees to be unlocked and to stay that way throughout the entire swing. The position we are looking for will cause your rear end to stick out a little and that is exactly what we want to happen. This will also help to prevent your weight from going forward to the toes.

Now that we have you in an athletic position from the hips down, we will address the back. Your back should be as straight as you can comfortably keep it. It may take a while to become comfortable with this, but it is well worth the time and effort because it is one of the keys to consistency. I haven't used the word consistency before. From now on we should be thinking not just about a good swing, but a consistent swing. My idea of a good consistent swing is a swing that, with practice, can be repeated time after time, without thinking of the parts of the swing. In other words, the swing should be automatic. The time that it takes to make a golf swing is so brief that you cannot think of the different parts of the swing while performing it. Anyone can achieve what I have described here, again, with patience and practice. There are no shortcuts, but the reward is huge.

THE GRIP

Now let's talk about the arms and hands. Starting with the grip, there are several acceptable ways to grip a golf club. The overlapping grip is the most popular. However, the interlocking grip has done pretty well for golfers with small hands, and to a lesser extent, the baseball grip with all ten fingers on the golf club. During the 1930s and early 1940s some golfers used a grip recommended by Alex Morrison a popular teacher of that era. Morrison's recommendation was an interlocking grip with the left thumb off of the club. Henry Picard, winner of the Masters Tournament in 1938, used this grip very effectively. I tried this grip and while it worked fairly well it cost me distance. I did best with the standard overlapping grip.

This overlapping grip is often referred to as the Vardon grip, named after the great Harry Vardon, who did not invent it but did make it popular. In the overlapping grip, the little finger on the right hand overlaps the forefinger of the left hand. I prefer to move it a little farther than a pure overlap. I like to place the small finger of my right hand on top of where the forefinger and middle finger of my left hand touch each other. While the kind of grip is not all important, it is important that the golfer does position his hands on the club correctly.

For a right-handed golfer this means that the back of the left hand should be facing the target with the left thumb placed slightly to the right of the top of the grip. The right hand is then placed on the club so that the left thumb fits into the hollow of the right hand. The "v" created by the thumb and forefinger of the right hand should point toward the right ear. The importance of a correct grip cannot be overemphasized. The grip is your only connection with the golf club and it determines the position of the face of the club at impact. Keep this in mind. The position of the back of the hand determines the way the club face is pointing *provided that the wrist does not hinge*. If the wrist hinges backward, a common fault, the face will open and the ball will go to the right. If, instead, you arch the left wrist, it will close the club face and a hook spin will be introduced.

It is important not to yield to the temptation of placing the right hand farther under the club just because it may feel stronger that way. This error could lead to smothered and/or low hooked shots. It also prevents the wrists from working as they should. If your shots have a tendency to go to the right, you may want to have the "V" formed by the thumb and finger of the right hand point a little more toward the right shoulder. Do not overdo this. Beware of a tendency to let the hands separate at the top of the backswing. The two hands must stay together on the grip throughout the entire golf swing, including the follow through. Although the ball is long gone by the time you get to the follow through, keeping the hands together is insurance against separating the hands before impact.

With regard to how hard to grip the club, it is important not to allow tension to set in. If the club is gripped too tightly, tension will spread to your wrists and arm muscles, as well. This will restrict the backswing and the release. Sam Snead once stated he gripped the club with the same amount of pressure that he would use if he were holding a bird, so that it couldn't get away, but neither would it be hurt. This may be a slight exaggeration but it does provide the idea of what kind of grip is needed if you are to have a smooth, flowing swing.

THE SETUP

In the address position, the golf ball should be situated about even with the left heel or instep when using a driver. The reason for this is that this position represents the bottom of the arc, for a properly executed downswing, after the weight has been shifted to the left side. When hitting irons, the ball should be positioned a little farther back, since we want to contact the golf ball while the clubhead is still descending. The idea with irons is to pinch the ball between the face of the iron and the ground.

With the straight back bent forward from the hips, the arms can be pretty much hanging down comfortably at address. Do not reach for the ball at address. The left arm should be straight without being rigid or stiff. The right arm should be bent at the elbow with the right elbow being comfortably close to the right hip. During practice it is a good idea to have the feeling that the bent right elbow is actually pointed toward the target. The reason that I emphasize this is that under no circumstance should the right elbow be allowed to move toward the rear during the backswing. If that happens it will prevent you from making a full turn away from the ball and you will start to arm swing. Ugh!

All of what has been described above is part of the setup. Take whatever time is necessary to get set up properly. Since the setup precedes the swing you can think about the details of the setup as you do it. Mentally, a golfer starts his golf swing as soon as he walks toward the ball to begin his setup. Consider that the setup is a part of the total swing and as important as any other part. You have probably noticed that any time a good player is disturbed after he begins his setup, he will walk away from the ball and start over. This is true for putting as well. It is very important. If your concentration is broken your chances of a good result are greatly diminished.

THE BACKSWING

Okay! You have learned to set up properly and are now ready to execute a full swing. Start the club back low and slow. You do not hit the ball with your backswing. A slow backswing will improve your chances for completing the backswing and then making a smooth transition to the downswing. By all means, avoid snatching the club backward. As you start the club back from the ball, try to keep your weight on the inside of your right foot. The importance of keeping your weight on the inside of your foot cannot be overemphasized. This will help you to make a proper turn with the upper part of the body, thereby avoiding the sway. Swaying is the worst enemy of the golf swing. Years ago, in order to train myself to make a proper turn, I placed golf balls under the outside of each foot just forward of the heel. Then, I made practice swings from that position, after which I hit golf balls under this same arrangement. It is next to impossible to sway when the outer edge of both shoes are raised as described here. As best you can, try to keep your hips from turning with your shoulders on the backswing. It will take some practice to become comfortable doing this, but it will become easier with time. Finally, you will get to the place where you do not have to think about doing it. It is well worth the effort.

When I was learning to play golf I decided to keep my left heel on the ground during the entire backswing. This was contrary to the way that Bobby Jones and Sam Snead played. It is my opinion that with their great talent they were able to play consistently despite lifting the left heel on the backswing. Today almost all of the touring professionals keep their left heel on the ground. This helps to restrict the hips from turning on the backswing and results in more body torque. Further, it means that there is one less moving part and this helps to make the swing compact and, therefore, easier to repeat.

It should be easy to understand the purpose of turning the shoulders without moving the hips. Visualize how this creates torque between the upper and lower parts of the body. The more torque you create, the faster your body will unwind, and this will create more clubhead speed. This is healthy power because it is accomplished without the use of the arms, but rather the use of the big muscles of the body. Take the club back as far as you can comfortably. If you are reasonably flexible, the shaft of a club as long as a driver or fairway club will be parallel to the ground at the top of the backswing. The right elbow position that was recommended for the setup will help you reach a good strong position at the top of the back swing. As you approach the top of the backswing, the right elbow may naturally come away from your side a little. If the elbow does come away from your side it should still be pointed toward the ground or a little forward. It should never be pointed to the rear.

You will notice that when you are in the address position, the back of the left hand is facing the target and is not hinged. Maintain that flat wrist position throughout the entire golf swing. In an attempt to get the club back far enough, there may be a tendency to let your left wrist hinge back. Avoid this at all cost because it will cause the face of the club to be open at impact. It is important to understand the difference between cocking the wrists and hinging them. Try this: place both hands, palms down on a table, and have both forearms also touching the table. While keeping the hands flat on the surface of the table, move the hands back and forth, to the left and then to the right, with no arm movement. This is a wrist cocking motion. Hinging is where you make a wrist movement perpendicular to the back of the hand (i.e. lifting your hands off the table). There is no place for this in a good golf swing.

It has been said that after his automobile accident, Ben Hogan used a little of this wrist hinging to prevent a hook and get a slight fade. This was referred to as "Hogan's Secret." There was a cover article about this in Life magazine back in the 1950s. In his case, however, the slightly hinged wrist position was maintained throughout the entire golf swing. I would not recommend that the average golfer try this. Hogan was unique and he was great. In his time, no one had more patience or practiced more than Ben Hogan.

Hogan wrote two books. The first one, *Power Golf*, was written early in his career. In the photos shown in this book, Hogan had a very long backswing with the shaft dipping far below horizontal at the top of his backswing. Since Hogan was quite small, this was probably a result of trying to get more distance. At that time, Hogan had a great deal of trouble trying to control a severe hook. In his second book about the five fundamentals, Hogan advocated an entirely different kind of swing, one that eliminated the possibility of the hook that had plagued him for so long.

THE DOWNSWING

The downswing is really quite simple. It had better be, because it consumes so little time.

And now comes the moment of truth! The downswing must be

initiated by the lower part of the body. This is *essential*. It will happen automatically if the weight has been maintained on the inside of the right foot during the backswing. Unless the lower part of the body moves first it is not possible for the clubhead to come into the ball from the inside. What we want to happen is for the clubhead to approach the ball from inside the line, travel along the line at impact, and then return to inside the line on the follow through. The only way to accomplish this is by shifting the weight, without moving your head, to the left foot at the start of the downswing. If, instead, the downswing is started with the shoulders and arms, the clubhead will come over the top and approach the ball from the outside. The ball would then travel on either a left to left flight path or a left to right slice will result, depending on the face position at impact. In neither case will the ball end up in the fairway.

The backswing I have described is the easiest way to go since the clubhead will follow pretty much the same path going back and coming down. A player can get away with a different kind of backswing, but then he must make a correction before he starts down. Jim Furyk is an example of someone who makes the recovery perfectly. In the past we have also seen this done by a few former tour players; Miller Barber and Gay Brewer come to mind. Each of these golfers started down with the weight transfer and immediately brought their right elbow into the side to obtain the delayed hit and an inside to out clubhead path. Remember then, start down with a transfer of the weight to the *inside* of the left foot, with your head held back. It is almost as if you are hitting into your side nearest to the target. This will automatically be accompanied by a turn of the hips to the left. Now there is room for the arms to come through without being blocked. Again, resist the temptation for the arms to be used at the beginning of the downswing. In fact, you should feel that they are not being used at all. From the top of the backswing until after you have transferred your weight to the leg nearer the target, the upper part of the body and both of the arms move as if they are one piece. Because the right elbow is pointing straight down, or slightly forward, as you shift your weight to the left side the right elbow will come into your side, automatically, and this is as it should be.

By the time you reach this point, centrifugal force will make your swing freewheeling and there is nothing left to do but release. If you have not used your arms at the beginning of the downswing your wrists will remain cocked and you will get the delayed hit that is so desirable. If you do make the mistake of using your arms it will force the wrists to uncock, which is the opposite of a delayed hit. It is called casting. When the weight is shifted to the left and your right elbow goes to your side, you will find yourself in a very strong position and, again, a late release of the clubhead will occur. The momentum of the club will pull the arms to the finish position. By this time the club will probably have pulled your weight to the outside of your left shoe. The release is really nothing more than the rotation of both of your hands and forearms as a unit, still making sure that the wrists are not permitted to hinge. Centrifugal force will make the wrists uncock without any effort on your part. Do this and the clubhead will square up at impact.

It is of utmost importance to keep your head behind the ball all through the downswing until the pull of the club on the follow through carries your head up with it. This may take some practice before it becomes second nature. The importance of keeping the head back long enough cannot be over emphasized. Some players, Jack Nicklaus is an example, turn or cock the head to the right just prior to taking the club back. This helps because by so doing the player's head has a greater distance to travel before it comes up and it provides added insurance against your head coming up early. If the head comes up too early, the club face will not square up at impact and this will result in a golf shot that is pushed to the right. I do not believe that any one actually "looks up" during the golf swing because they are concentrating on the ball. The head usually comes up early because the right shoulder drives it up due to a faulty swing, one with the right shoulder getting into the act too early.

The only time that the two arms are straight at the same time is shortly after impact. By this time the ball has already separated from the clubhead. However, the two arms being straight at that time is a sign that a good swing has been made. The same applies to the follow through. When a golfer finishes in a well balanced position you know that he made a good, balanced swing and kept his head back long enough.

THE DELAYED HIT

A little earlier I referred to a delayed hit. You might ask why a delayed hit is so desirable. There are two very good reasons. The first is that the body can turn back to the ball faster if the club is maintained in a cocked position during the early part of the downswing. While the wrists are cocked during the early part of the downswing, the clubhead remains close to the axis about which the body is turning. Therefore the entire system has a much smaller moment of inertia and can achieve a greater rotational acceleration. This will result in greater clubhead speed, which translates into greater distance. It is easy to understand why the greater rotational acceleration takes place if you think of an example that I will use again later. This is the case of a figure skater who wants to spin. The skater wraps his arms around his body in order to decrease his moment of inertia. This results in a greater spin rate. When the skater wants to slow the spin he releases his arms and stretches them outward. This increases the moment of inertia and slows the spin rate.

The second advantage of the delayed hit is that the radius of the swing arc at the time when impact occurs is much smaller if the release is delayed. If the wrists uncock early, the radius of the swing is the combined length of the arms and the golf club. In a delayed hit, the radius of the swing is merely the length of the golf club. This changes the angle of attack of the clubhead with respect to ball and this, in turn, will impart more backspin to the ball. More backspin means more lift and more lift means more carry, or hang time. A ball struck with an iron using a delayed hit swing will hold the green better and may even backup when using a lofted club. You have probably observed the difference in trajectory when a golf ball is hit by a touring pro as compared to the average handicap golfer. This is due to the delayed hit. The path of the ball for the high handicap golfer will follow more of a parabolic path, with its apex about half way to the target. When struck by a good golfer, the ball reaches its zenith much closer to the target. It sort of planes its way to the highest point and drops more steeply. That is the kind of golf ball trajectory that will hold a green.

PRACTICE

This may sound like a lot to think about, and it is. But the place to think about this is while you are sitting in an arm chair or on the practice range, not while you are on the golf course. On the course, limit your thoughts to no more than one key during each swing. Allow the habits you have developed on the practice tee to work for you. When you are practicing try whatever new changes you want to make, but do them one at a time. Once you feel comfortable with a particular change, then go to the next change you want to make.

To a person observing a good golfer making a golf swing, it will probably appear that the golfer is swinging his arms in order to execute the swing. This just is not the case. It is not the case for the discus thrower and it is not the case for a good golfer. Certainly a golf ball can be hit using the arms; however, both distance and accuracy would suffer. If you develop the golf swing described here, you can improve and you will end up with a good, repeating golf swing. From a mechanical standpoint it is not only the best way to go, it is also the most simple because there are less moving parts to coordinate. If at present you are a high handicap golfer, you now have the opportunity to change and improve your game significantly. Remember, it takes patience and practice. There is no substitute.

Back around 1950, when I was working on my game I did not have the benefit of a driving range. I practiced in the evening, when the golf course was not occupied. I had to supply my own golf balls and then pick them up as well. My shag bag always contained the same brand of golf balls. Then I could be sure when

I had finally reached consistency with a certain club. I eventually reached a point where I could hit full wedge shots to a blanket. When I was playing I always expected to be inside of fifteen feet with a wedge or nine iron. It was a nice feeling. Of course it didn't always come out that way, but nine out of ten isn't bad.

EQUIPMENT

At this point we will discuss matters that concern the golfer besides the golf swing—namely, equipment, clothes, and accessories.

On the subject of selecting golf clubs, it is obvious that being fitted with clubs that suit you and your golf swing is of the utmost importance. There are a number of electronic aids available today that will measure the clubhead speed as well as other characteristics of the golf swing. Most golf shops have this kind of equipment available. This is the best way to decide on the shaft that suits you best. The suitable shaft stiffness as it is related to clubhead speed will be found elsewhere in this book.

Unless you are a low handicap golfer I recommend perimeter-weighted irons. They are more forgiving for off-center hits. Also, if you are a beginner or high handicap golfer you might consider clubs with offset heads. If you improve over time, and I am confident that you will, you can then switch to muscle-back irons and clubs without offset heads.

There is one feature about golf clubs that is rarely discussed. I refer to the matter of the lie that is built into the golf club. When a golfer lines up his shot he is supposed to have the lower edge of the club face perpendicular to the line of flight he has chosen. If the club is soled properly, with a good swing the ball will travel along the selected target line. When a golfer buys a set of clubs, the golfer will usually find that he doesn't have a choice with regard to the lie of the clubs. The lie of a golf club is the angle that the shaft makes with the sole of the club. Some golfers carry their hands low at address, Hubie Green is an example. Others carry their hands high. The clubs that are available in the shop may have been made for the average man or woman. Are you that average?

This is not a serious matter when it comes to irons, because irons can usually have the lies altered by having them bent at a golf club repair shop. It is important to have the lies of your clubs suit your unique physical characteristics at the address position. The reason for going into so much detail on this is that if the club is not properly soled the ball may go to the right or left of the target line, depending on the way the club sits. If the toe is off the ground at address the face will actually be facing left and the target will be missed on that side. This is the reason that golf shots off side-hill lies, with the ball above your feet, will normally miss the target to the left.

The opposite is true if the heel of the club is off the ground at address. Some years ago I made a model to demonstrate this. I took a six iron and drilled a hole perpendicular to the face of the club, through a point near the sweet spot. I cut a thread in the hole and screwed a threaded steel rod in it. When the sole of the six iron was properly soled, the steel rod pointed directly along the target line. If I lowered the grip end of the club, still keeping the bottom edge of the club face at right angle to the target line, the rod pointed well to the left of the target. The reverse occurred if I tipped the club so that the heel was off the ground. Then the rod pointed to the right. Caution: do not allow errors built into your clubs to affect your game. Make certain that your golf clubs fit you.

I dislike the word "average." It does have its place and use, but you must know if it is being used in a useful manner. When I was teaching I used an example to demonstrate how the word "average" can be practically meaningless. I asked the students, "If there were 50 people in a room and 25 of them were exactly 20 years old and 25 of them were exactly 60 years old, what is the average age? Of course, the mathematical average is 40 years old, yet no one in the room was within 20 years of the average age. Moral: Make certain that your golf clubs fit you, not the average man or woman.

In selecting metal woods, do not waste your money on thin-faced titanium clubs unless you are sure that you can benefit from this feature. Your clubhead speed is the determining factor if you hit the ball squarely. If your clubhead speed with a driver is less than 90 miles per hour, you will not get much, if any, benefit from titanium clubheads. Stainless steel clubs may be half as expensive.

When looking for a driver you will find that there are different lofts from which to choose, a range of seven degrees to twelve degrees. If you do not find what you want, go to another shop. I recommend that beginners and senior golfer use drivers with greater loft, as much as twelve degrees. The fact that beginners and seniors do not develop as much clubhead speed means that their ball will not have as much backspin as a stronger golfer develops. The added loft helps to make up for this. Neither of these two classes of golfers benefit from high volume titanium drivers.

As for putters, that is really an individual matter. Certainly, a putter with a large moment of inertia is helpful for every golfer. These putters are more forgiving on off-center contacts. However, the swing with a putter is so short that an off-center hit is much less likely to occur than when taking a full golf swing. Try a few putters until you find one that is pleasing to your eyes as you address the putt; it will give you more confidence.

In my own case, I never did well with a mallet putter. Because of what I used fifty years ago, my eyes still like the looks of a modified blade putter. The modified blade is still quite popular today. Recently I have seen a great many new exotic putters on the tour. Then again I saw one tour player using a Wilson 8802 putter that must be fifty to sixty years old.

It is a good idea to locate the sweetspot on your putter. One way that you can do this is to suspend the putter, or any other golf club, at the butt end with two fingers. Hold it lightly enough so that the club is free to swing. Using a golf tee or a small coin, tap the face of the putter near where you think the sweetspot might be. Trying different spots in that general area you will find one place where no clubhead twist occurs and where you do not feel a force applied to the two fingers holding the club. That point is the sweetspot or center of percussion. I have seen putters which had grooves at the top to indicate the sweetspot and found that it was actually elsewhere. It is worth locating the sweetspot on the putter even if it is center-shafted.

Since the player's grip on the club is so important, most golfers wear a glove on the hand that is applied to the top of the club. Right-handed golfers wear a glove on the left hand. If you practice a great deal a glove is a must. Wearing a glove is also easier on the club grips, and helps to make the grips last longer. The grip on the club should feel "tacky." If the oil from your skin makes the grips slick, clean them, if you can, or replace them. You may notice that caddies for the touring pros carry a wet towel to clean the clubhead and the grip after each shot.

Golf shoes should be comfortable and large enough so that you can wear heavy socks. Heavy socks will absorb moisture and keep you comfortable through the entire round. Examine the spikes on your shoes regularly. Most courses now require that the golfers use soft spikes rather than steel spikes. Soft spikes wear down rather quickly due to walking on the pavement between the clubhouse and the golf course. The firmness of your stance depends on the spikes. Make sure that they are in good enough condition so that your feet will not slip during a full swing.

If there is any chance that you may play in the rain, carry an umbrella and rain gear in your golf bag. Of course the umbrella will help to keep you dry. The ribs of the umbrella can also serve as a rack to keep a towel dry and it can do the same for your golf glove, if you take it off when you putt. You should remove your golf glove to give added sensitivity to your hands when putting. During tournaments, I always carried two extra gloves in my golf bag, just in case. A wet golf glove is worse than no golf glove. All of these matters I am discussing are important because they help to prevent distractions during play.

I may say this more than once because it is important enough to warrant repeating: After you have planned your strategy on a hole, never think about anything but the golf shot you are about to hit. You cannot do anything about the last shot and you certainly cannot play a future shot until you get to it.

Golf is fun. Good golf is even more fun!

THE SHORT GAME—LOWER YOUR SCORE

If a person is just starting to learn to play golf, I would recommend learning to play golf from the hole back. It probably goes against human nature for a male adult to go at the game this way. The average man starts with the driver, which is the most difficult club to master. Unfortunately, many teachers contribute to this mistake. When you do this, you are trying to run before you learn to walk. Many of us are responsible for initiating our children to the game. I recommend that those who do start the youngsters in this fashion, short game first. I started to teach golf to my son when he was about six. I didn't allow Tom on the golf course for the first two years. We practiced together and then later played a great deal of golf together. My most precious memories are the father and son tournaments we played in while Tom was growing up.

What I am recommending makes a lot of sense when you consider the objective. Most full size courses have a par of 72, plus or minus two. The most shots struck with any one club are the putts. Par 72 represents an ideal game, without flukes, where a golfer hits 18 greens in regulation. This represents 36 strokes. The other 36 strokes are taken as putts: two putts per green.

PUTTING

If putting is half the game for a good golfer, it makes sense to place the greatest emphasis on putting. A golfer with an eighteen handicap will average sixty percent of his strokes on and around the green. Based on these facts, for a beginner, putting should be the starting point, followed by chipping. Putting is certainly the easiest thing for a youngster to do. Starting with the short game will help to build confidence. A youngster can start putting shortly after he or she is able to walk confidently. I believe that Tiger Woods was about two when I first saw him putt, from about six inches, on the Ed Sullivan Show. Another good reason for starting children when they are young is that a child can learn rapidly and is also a first-class mimic. I recall that at the Morgantown Country Club we had an eleven-year-old caddy who could imitate the golf swing of every member of the club.

Putting is an individual matter. If you watch the players on the PGA Tour, you will observe a great many different methods employed, as well as different kinds of putters being used. Putting is a delicate and sensitive procedure, especially on fast greens. A strong golfer is called upon to hit a drive 300 yards and then, a few minutes later, is required to baby a downhill putt on a very slick green. It is easy to understand that this can be very hard on the nerves. In fact, putting has been the cause of many older golfers quitting competitive golf. Before they do quit they will try almost anything that might allow them to putt without having the yips.

At one time some of them tried croquet-style putting. This worked pretty well, until the United Stats Golf Association put an end to that by introducing a rule requiring that both feet be on the same side of the line of the putt. Sam Snead was one of the few who continued with a variation of the croquet principle. He putted with both feet together on one side of the putting line still facing the target as in croquet. His right hand gripped the shaft just above the hosel of the putter. This method became known as side-saddle putting.

The long putter has since been introduced and has not been legislated against, so far. A newer variation is the belly putter. This putter, shorter than the long putter, keeps the butt end of the putter anchored against the body near the belt area. Otherwise it is used the same as a regular putter.

It makes sense to learn and perfect the short game first. In the first place it is easier to make short shots, particularly putting and chipping. Again, it helps develop confidence. It also helps to develop touch, a great asset to anyone's golf game. Despite the differences in putting grips and the kinds of putters used, there are a few things that all good putters do. I like to refer to them as fundamentals.

It is of paramount importance to keep the head and lower body perfectly still while putting. You cannot become a good, consistent putter unless you do this. Most good putters also keep hand motion completely out of their putting strokes. The reason for this is that hand movements complicate the putting stroke by changing the direction that the putter head is facing during the stroke. There have been many players in the past that were good putters even though they were wrist putters. It was even said that Bobby Locke, probably the best putter of his day, hooked his putts. It makes sense, though, to try do develop the most simple style because it is the easiest to repeat.

The majority of the golfers that we see on the tour use putters that are approximately 35 inches long. They employ a shoulder motion with the wrists pretty much locked. It is a pendulum-type motion. The face of the putter is always perpendicular to the line that was chosen. The setup requires that the back be comfortably bent and that you maintain a steady, light, grip on the putter. The reason for the light grip is that it prevents the arm and shoulder muscles from becoming tight. If these muscles become tight, then your touch, or sensitivity, is lost. A good putter does not hit the putt. He allows the putter head to do the work. With a light touch you can feel the putter head. If you follow these principles, with practice you will develop a feel for the length of the putting stroke required to accommodate the distance called for on each putt.

Putting is further complicated by the slopes and undulations you will encounter on the greens. Rarely will you have a perfectly level putt. Uphill putts are much easier to play than any other type. For this reason, trying to keep the ball below the hole is part of the strategy when playing into a green. I remember playing an interclub match some years ago at my course, Lakeview Country Club, near Morgantown, West Virginia. The fourth hole, a three par, had a steep slope at the narrow front part of the skull-shaped green. My opponent hit a nice iron shot to a spot four feet above the hole. His birdie putt lipped out and his ball ran completely off the front of the green. He had to chip for his third shot. This can make a golfer age in a hurry.

It might be best to start with a grip where the two hands are directly opposite each other with both thumbs on top of the grip. A player may find another way to put his hands onto the club that suits him better. Unlike a full golf swing, the reason that the putting grip is not all important is that the hands and the wrists do not flex during the putt. The shoulders do all the work. Another benefit of this type of putting motion is that the putter stays low the ground throughout the putting stroke and this helps the putter head to contact the ball more squarely each time. This is a good thing to keep in mind when playing on slow greens, where a longer putting stroke is required. Try to think of the putting stroke as a swing rather than a hit. If you think of swinging the putter, you will allow the weight of the putter do all the work and the distance the ball travels will be determined by the length of the backswing. When doing this, the follow through will be almost the same length as the backswing. On something as delicate as a putt on a fast green, it is very difficult to gauge how hard to "hit" a ball. That is why I emphasize that you let the weight of the head of the putter do the work for you.

I am not going to go into the matter of reading the greens. This has so many variables, every green being different, that the golfer can best learn from experience. You will know instinctively about playing the break of a putt due to the undulations on the green. Only experience can teach you how much break to play. This part of putting is not difficult to learn, but it is time consuming. If you are playing in the southern states you may run into golf courses that have Bermuda grass greens. Most clubs try to have bent grass for their greens. The heat and humidity experienced in southern United States make it next to impossible for them to use bent grass. The matter of maintenance expense is also a factor in choosing the kind of grass for the greens. I mention all this because putting on Bermuda grass greens can be different from putting on bent grass. Depending on the location, Bermuda greens will go dormant in the winter and turn yellow. Then it is necessary to overseed the greens with blue grass for the late fall, winter, and early spring.

Another factor in putting is the matter of grain. Grass does not grow straight up. The combination of the effect of the sun and drainage contribute to grain on the putting surface. Putting into the grain is much slower than putting with the grain. You can sometimes determine the direction of the grain by the color of the grass. Looking down grain the putting surface will appear lighter and perhaps more shiny than it does looking at it from the opposite direction. At the hole you can see the grain by examining the grass around the rim of the hole. Since the cup liner is an inch below the putting surface the direction in which the grass is leaning is readily apparent. If you are putting on a line that is neither directly with or against the grain, the putt will curve in the direction that the grain is leaning.

I recall some years ago when I played the West Course of the Broadmoor Hotel in Colorado Springs. The greens were very fast and grain was a major factor for both determining the line of the putt and the speed. I soon learned to look where the mountains were before lining up a putt. It helped me a great deal in reading that putt. Golfers who have played oceanside courses know that on the greens the ball will break toward the ocean. Even wind can be a factor, although it must be quite windy for this to happen. When playing in Hawaii on one occasion, it was so windy that the ball at rest on the putting surface was actually vibrating. In that type of situation it is important that you do not ground your putter when addressing the putt. If you do ground your putter and the ball moves you are responsible for having made the ball move and you will incur a penalty. In Hawaii I had to allow for the wind on every putt. Birdies were hard to come by that day.

You may choose to putt from off the green for various reasons. This will occur most frequently when you are on the fringe, the first cut of grass, around the green. However, there are occasions where you are still on the short grass in the fairway, yet a fairly short distance from the green. The problem usually occurs when you need to come into a green with a short pin location and there isn't much green to work with. Putting may offer the best chance of getting the ball close to the hole. When playing at the Old Course at St. Andrews, I found it best to putt from a much farther distance from the green. The fairway grass is so dense and tight that chipping is quite risky. If a person does choose to chip he must be certain to play the ball forward, take the ball cleanly, not allowing the chipping club to stub itself on the unforgiving turf. On a full shot, the speed of the clubhead will easily penetrate the turf. But the turf at some courses, such as the Old Course at St. Andrews, are unforgiving to a short chipping or pitching stroke that is not picked cleanly.

CHIPPING VS. PITCHING

A chipping stroke can be made two different ways. It is a good idea to have both in your inventory. If you must chip when you are a very short distance from the putting green, you can employ the same technique as you do when putting. If practical, chip the ball onto the green as close to the near edge of green as you can safely, and let it roll the rest of the way to the hole. If the circumstances are such that you cannot chip the ball to land on the putting surface, I recommend chipping with a club that has little loft. This will minimize the amount of backspin and prevent the ball from hanging up in the taller grass.

The remaining stroke that makes up the short game is the pitch shot. The pitch shot is struck with a lofted club because it is necessary to avoid some obstacle that lies between the ball and the green. The obstacle may be a bunker or a patch of rough. Use the pitch shot only as a last resort. Because the pitch shot is a made with a short stroke it is difficult to impart much backspin to the golf ball. I am sure that you have seen some of the experts hit a very short shot, using a sixty or sixty-four degree wedge, and taking what looks like a full swing. It is a beautiful thing to watch but I do not advise any player to try this shot without having had sufficient practice to master it.

The pitch shot appears to be a miniature version of a full swing.

It differs from the chip in that the pitch shot requires considerable use of the arms and hands. The pitch shot is somewhat like the lower part of the full swing, except that much less body movement is required because of the abbreviated backswing. The pitch is a finesse shot. If you need the ball to stop rather quickly, you may want to keep the face of the club open throughout the swing, including the follow through. Since there is less body movement it is a good idea to alter your address position from that of a full shot, and set up with an open stance where the left foot is pulled back considerably and you are partially facing the hole. The open stance keeps your hips out of the way so that they will not block the shot. Since this is a more delicate shot, the feet should be fairly close together in the address position. Optimally, this is a soft shot and the grip should be lighter than it is for a full shot. I like to think, "soft shot, soft hands," as I get ready to hit a pitch. Load your mind with what you want to do before hitting the pitch, and every other shot as well. I recall that when I was faced with the kind of trouble shot on which I needed to get the ball up quickly to clear some trees, I thought about what I had to do and then I would automatically keep my weight back a little more in order to accomplish this. I can assure you that a lot of golf is played in the five inches between your ears. Let me repeat: practice breeds confidence and confidence leads to success.

BUNKER SHOTS

There are two kinds of bunker shots. The fairly short bunker shot from around a green is played differently from the method used for fairway bunkers. When playing from fairway bunkers it is essential to hit the ball first. From bunkers around the green the player does not want to hit the ball at all. For these shots the clubhead enters the sand behind the ball and passes under it. The sand that is displaced lifts and moves the golf ball. To prevent the sand wedge from digging too deep, the sand wedge is equipped with a flange, sometimes referred to as the bounce. For sand shots that are intended to have backspin, a player will take a shallow layer of sand beneath the ball.

When addressing a sand shot the player should assume an open stance and open the face of the sand wedge. This will not send the ball to the right because it is the sand that moves the ball. It is important to have the clubhead go through the shot. Do not quit as the sand is encountered.

Occasionally a player will have the misfortune of hitting a ball into the bunker and the ball will stay in the depression it made when it landed. You have now been introduced to the "fried egg." The ball is in the center of a small crater. With practice you can learn to get the ball out of this type of lie every time. The clubhead must enter the sand at a point further back from the ball than when hitting from a clean lie, just behind the edge of the crater made by the ball. For such a shot the face of the club should not be laid open as much because you want the club to penetrate deeper in order to get under the ball. You might practice this shot with a pitching wedge or 60 degree wedge that does not have bounce. The final choice will depend on the kind of sand and its condition. You can judge the quality of the sand as you set your feet for the bunker shot. The rules of golf do not permit the golfer to test the sand. However, the information gained from fairly taking your stance is not a violation of the rules. One thing that you want to be sure to do is to go through the shot and have a follow through.

A player is entitled to see part of the ball before playing a bunker shot. Occasionally, the player may hit a ball into the face of a bunker, where it then becomes completely covered by sand. The rules allow the player to move enough sand to enable him to see the top of the ball before making his stroke.

There will be occasions when you must get the ball up more quickly because of the shape and/or the depth of the bunker. This is a common situation on many courses in Scotland and in pot bunkers in this country. Some of the older courses also have very deep bunkers. St Louis Country Club, where the Snead /Worsham U.S. Open showdown occurred, is a course that has some of these. In this type of situation you should think of making the swing more of a "V" shape rather than a "U" shape. When the swing and follow through are steeper the ball will come up more abruptly.

Bunker shots are made to look easy by the touring pros, and the short ones are easy for them. I remember watching U.S. Opens where a missed green might leave a situation that would be very difficult to handle. In this case a player may intentionally aim for a bunker, leaving him a much easier shot to save par. When we watch professionals play in a golf tournament the bunkers almost always have sand that is in good condition and fairly easy to manage. On the other hand, municipal courses and the golf courses at some private clubs may have sand that has become packed. This is where a player must learn to improvise. There are times when it may be wiser to leave the sand wedge in the golf bag. Remember, golf is a game of "how many," not "how."

It is ideal if you can have someone check what you are working on during practice sessions. It is dangerous to practice the wrong thing and make a habit of this error. Of course, the way your ball behaves after you strike it should tell you something. Every time you practice make sure you have a clear plan in mind as to what you want to accomplish that day. For every golf shot that you hit at the practice range, you should have a target and trajectory in mind. Do not just go out and hit golf balls. That is exercise, not golf practice.

One of the major reasons why a player cannot take his game from the practice range to the golf course is that when he is hitting the same club repeatedly, he can make an adjustment to compensate for what the golf ball might be doing at that time. When he goes to the golf course he is no longer hitting the same shot again and again. Each shot is different. This is why I have emphasized consistency.

THINKING YOUR WAY
AROUND THE GOLF COURSE

Many a good golfer does not score as well as he should. The reason for this may not lie in his golf swing but rather that he exercised poor judgment in how to play some of the holes. Just as in football, a good game plan is required for golf. Planning your golf strategy is easier than planning football strategy because in football the other team may come up with surprises. Football coaches always spend hours studying films of the opposing team. However, the coach does not have any idea but that the opposing team may play differently than they did the week or two before. The one thing that a golf game and a football game do have in common is that strategy is required for both. There are certain principles that you should follow regardless of what golf course you are going to play. First, play each hole in a manner that takes advantage of your golf game's best features. Second, attack the weaknesses of the golf course.

PUTTING YOURSELF IN GOOD POSITIONS

A player is the best judge of what is the strongest part of his or her game. Try to put your ball in a position that will allow you to use the shot that you like best to hit. I recall when my son Tom and I played in the St. Louis District father and son golf tournaments. Tom was an excellent driver of the golf ball. However, his iron play left something to be desired. The format for these events was selective drive; pick up one ball and hit alternate shots thereafter. We would try to use Tom's drive on the par four holes so that I could hit the iron shot into the green. On the par fives we would plan to use my drive. After Tom made the second shot, I would again be in a position to hit the shot to the green. This arrangement worked very well for us in all of the tournaments in which we played. We were able to use our individual strengths on each hole.

When you reach the teeing ground, look down the fairway to see if there is any trouble present on that hole. If there is trouble on just one side of the fairway, tee your ball on the same side of the teeing ground as the trouble. The reason for this may be purely psychological; however, it does give you a more comfortable feeling of hitting away from trouble. It is a win-win situation.

Before you hit any tee shot, look to see what the approach to the green looks like. Aim the tee shot toward a location that will make your approach to the green a safer shot. Quite often you will find that the opening to the green is not aligned with the center of the fairway. There may be a bunker guarding one side of the green and by placing your tee shot in a particular place it takes the bunker out of play and opens the hole for you. This is not too different from the situation one encounters when shooting pool. In pool, after you select the target pocket, you plan for the next shot. You then hit the cue ball in such a manner that it will end up in a good place for the next shot.

If you are not a good sand player I would recommend that you do not attempt to reach a green with a golf shot that requires the use of a long club. You will be better off to play your approach shot short of the trouble and try to get up and down from there. The worst you will probably get is a bogey. If you have a decent short game you will make par more often than not. When you gamble you are in danger of making a double bogey or worse. This is especially true for a hole that has water on one side of the green and bunkers on the other side.

Your strategy may be different depending on whether you are playing in a match play or stroke play competition. In match play it doesn't make any difference if you lose a hole by one stroke or four strokes. However, in stroke play all your mistakes stay with you throughout the entire event. When you are involved in a stroke play competition take only those kinds of shots that you are confident that you can hit successfully. Do not try a shot that you *hope* you can make.

If you must lay up on a hole it is best to lay up in a manner that will leave you with the kind of shot that is easiest for you. This will occur quite frequently when you must lay up on a hole that has water in front of the green. It is usually better to leave yourself with a full pitching wedge or sand wedge shot rather than a part shot. I know that I would much rather have a full shot of 100 to 110 yards than a part shot of 50 yards. From 110 yards I can take a full swing and I can put more spin on the ball.

If you need to hit your tee shot to a narrow fairway bordered by heavy rough, consider hitting something other than a driver. You will be much better off with a ball that stays in the fairway than you will be if you end up with a longer drive that comes to rest in the deep rough or in the trees.

One of the most difficult shots in golf is a long bunker shot from around the green. Wherever possible, select a strategy that will avoid this type of situation. A lay up is a far better decision. Fairway bunker shots are no bargain but they are not very difficult if you have a decent lie. The all-important part of a fairway bunker shot is to play the ball far enough back so that you will strike the ball before you contact the sand. The sand that you take on this shot, like a divot on the fairway, should be in front of where the ball was.

You should always try to hit a shot into the green in such a manner as to leave it below the hole. This is especially important when you are playing a course that has fast greens. Not only will it help to make more birdies, but it will also help you avoid a three-putt green.

PLAYING FROM THE ROUGH

Then there is the matter of playing a golf shot from the rough. Is it any different from hitting a ball from the fairway? The answer is, "yes." How much different depends on the nature of the rough. If the rough is fairly long, and the ball settles down in the grass, the grass will come between the clubhead and the ball at impact. You have probably heard the expression, "He can't get the club on the ball." If this is the case you cannot predict the outcome. One thing is certain, though—the ball will not have the usual backspin that you expect when hitting from a clean lie. You cannot expect it to hold a green. At times you may get a flyer and the ball will travel ten to twenty yards farther than you expected to hit it with that club. Unless you are very strong the best thing to do is take your medicine and use whatever club you know will get you out of that deep rough. Repeat: a club you *know* will get you out of that deep rough. The last thing you need is to still be in the deep rough for the next shot. If necessary aim for the fairway instead of the green.

The most extreme example of this that I ever encountered first hand took place during a West Virginia Open that I played in some years back. The tournament was held at Williams Country Club located in Weirton, West Virginia. Williams Country Club was owned by Weirton Steel and it was a player-friendly course that was always kept in beautiful condition. The fairways and the greens were composed of bent grass. Most of the players in the tournament were club professionals from West Virginia. Before the tournament some of the pros had teased the host professional, telling Monty how they were going to "tear the course apart" during the event.

Quite some time before the tournament, the fairways were narrowed to less than thirty yards and the first cut of rough was watered and allowed to grow. The rough adjoining the fairways was now bent grass that would stand 8 to 12 inches long if it were able to stand vertically. The already fast greens were allowed to get quite dry and then rolled with a heavy water roller. It was a nightmare. On the first day I played with three club professionals and I shot 85. I was the low man in our group. The next day I did a little better and was one over par on one of the nines. After play each day, the ground crew would run through the rough with a tractor dragging a large, stiff wire loop. The wire loop picked up the tall bent grass in the rough and curled it, just in case some of it had been stepped on while looking for a ball or playing a shot the day before. I found that the longest club that I could use effectively in that rough was a seven iron. If a player hit a really bad shot that went beyond the bent grass rough to the regular rough, he didn't have much of a problem unless there were trees in his line. From this location a player could use almost any club in his bag. It didn't seem fair that a player was penalized severely only if he barely missed the cut fairway but not if the golf shot was worse. The club pros were in shock. What would the home folk think when they saw that their club pro had a tough time breaking 90?

I have thought of this at some of the U.S. Opens where course conditions somewhat resembled the conditions at Williams Country Club. This makes the players leave their titanium drivers in their golf bags on most of the holes. Instead of adding length to the course, all that is needed is to narrow the fairways and let the rough grow for tournaments. You wouldn't keep the course like that for the members at a club where the average handicap is about 18; if you did scores would zoom and the game would take much longer due to time required to look for golf balls in the deep rough. On this subject, I find it peculiar that all the fuss is about something that affects only the touring pros and very low handicap golfers: a small minority of the total golf population. Yet, the USGA continues to make rules that affect millions of higher handicap golfers.

"TEE IT HIGH AND LET IT FLY"

Learn to tee your ball for a drive at the right height for your swing. The object is to hit the ball on the so-called sweet spot. If you miss the sweet spot toward the toe or heel, you will lose both distance and direction. The same is true for making contact too high or too low on the club face. In either of these cases you will hit the ball either too high or too low and lose distance. A good way to determine what height is best for you is on the practice tee, where you can use wooden tees. There are several ways to do this. The first is using some special adhesive tape that you can apply to the face of your driver. This special tape will clearly show where the impact occurred on the face of the driver. I have even seen this done successfully using masking tape. Another method is to apply talcum powder to the ball. After impact, there will be an easily recognizable dimple pattern on the club face where contact was made. With this evidence you can make whatever adjustments are necessary to do a better job of teeing the ball and make better contact more often. This is important. If you are using a fairway wood off the tee, set the ball lower in order to get the ball on the sweet spot of that thinner-faced club.

GAMESMANSHIP

I would like to spend a little space here on the subject of gamesmanship. Beware! You are most apt to run into this during match play because you have just one opponent. However, there are circumstances in which this may occur during a stroke play competition, as well, especially late in the round or during the last round of a multi-day event. There are a great many ways that your opponent may try to get to you, or to get into your head, so to speak. One way may be by altering the pace of play. If your opponent notices that you are a fast player he may slow down in an effort to make you antsy. Believe me, this has been done. I knew of a member in my club who "had to lie down and rest for awhile." During a match. It was not just a coincidence that he was three down at the time. Another way to get into a player's head is by way of compliments. For example, "You have one of the smoothest, most deliberate backswings I have ever seen." Your opponent is trying to make you conscious of the way you swing, which would, of course, spoil your concentration. Or your opponent may say: "I don't see how anyone is going to be able to beat you in this tournament." Again, beware!

Walter Hagen was said to be the best at this. There is one story that demonstrates his gamesmanship best. Because he was such an excellent shot maker he would try to throw his opponent off on club selection. The story that I relate here took place during a PGA tournament that at that time was played at match play. On a par three hole that would normally require the use of a five iron, Hagen had the honor. Instead of the five iron that the golf shot called for, he selected a three iron, making certain that his opponent was aware of the club he had selected. He then took something off the shot and reached the green short of the pin. His opponent then also selected a three iron and hit his ball 20 yards over the green. This is the epitome of gamesmanship.

I was the victim of this tactic by someone I didn't even play with that day. One year when I was trying to qualify for the USGA Senior Amateur, the qualifying event was held at Old Warson Country Club in Ladue, Missouri. The USGA representative in charge of the qualifying was a former Walker Cup player who was also in the field. There were only two slots open for golfers in this regional qualifying event. The contestants were permitted a practice round on the Friday preceding the Monday qualifying round. In my group for the Friday practice round was this former Walker Cup player. I had a good game that day and finished the practice round with a score of 71, one under par. This was low score in my group. On Monday, I arrived at Old Warson about an hour ahead of my tee time in order to warm up on the practice range and to hit a few putts. When I arrived, Bob told me that he had to make some changes and I was now scheduled to be on the tee in less than ten minutes. I was steamed. Needless to say, I didn't qualify that year. Shame on me! However, the next year I was better prepared and did qualify for the event. Yes, gamesmanship can show up in many ways.

PLAYING IN WIND

When playing on a day when there is an appreciable amount of wind you have something extra to think about on every shot. If the wind is against you the ball will climb higher than usual, allowing the wind to have more time to work on the ball. You may have a one club wind or a two club wind. The ball will climb higher and come down rather steeply without much roll, if any. When hitting into the wind, it is a good idea to play the ball a little farther back in your stance. This effectively takes some loft off the club and a lower ball trajectory will result. The opposite is true if you have a trailing wind. The ball will not climb as high but it will still travel farther and have less spin. This ball will roll after it hits the ground. With a trailing wind you may not be able to keep a ball on a closely guarded green. In this case use a more lofted club, which will help you hit the ball higher, and thereby compensate for the tail wind. If there is a strong wind coming from either side, this is a good time to pray and then lay up. It takes practice to know just how much to allow for the side wind. To complicate things further, the wind may not be steady throughout the flight of the ball or the wind may be different near the green. Even the touring professionals suffer under these conditions. Average scores may go up three or four strokes, even for the best players on a very windy day on a tight course. There will not be many birdies on a day like this. Any birdies made on that day are probably lucky because the player was not intending to gamble. When I use the word "lucky," I refer to something like a hole in one. I know; I've had five. At one time players used balls with different kinds of markings for different holes, depending on the wind direction. This is no longer permitted.

There will be occasions in which you must improvise as you play. For example, when playing in Scotland you may encounter sand bunkers that have sides that are nearly vertical. You may also run into this on a Pete Dye course, where railroad ties are used to shore up the face of a bunker. If your ball stops against a vertical wall, it may be impossible to hit the ball in the direction of your target. If you declare an unplayable lie you must still leave the ball in the bunker. Therefore, the sensible choice may be to hit the ball sideways and pay your dues. Since these situations cannot be predicted, improvisation is the order of the day.

The worst case of course management that I have ever witnessed occurred during the 1999 British Open at Carnoustie. The French player Jean Van de Velde went to the tee of the par four 72nd hole with a three-stroke lead. He knew that a two over par six would win the tournament. His first mistake was taking a driver instead of an iron or fairway club off the tee. He hit the driver to the right, where it almost went into a stream but came to rest on the 17th fairway. Instead of laying up short he went all out for a blind green. He hit another bad shot and ended up in deep rough in front of the grandstand. Hitting from grass up to his knees he hit his next shot into the burn (creek) just a few yards in front of him. He had a sheer-faced wall in front of him. This time, though, he did take a penalty drop. His fifth shot, needing to hole out to win, landed in the greenside bunker. His sixth shot was a decent bunker shot to about five feet. He holed out his seventh shot.

THE RULES OF GOLF

Know the rules of golf. By now the rules are the same for the USGA and the Royal and Ancient Club of St. Andrews. This was not always the case. The purpose of the rules is to make the game fair for everyone. Ignorance of the rules can result in disqualification during a tournament. If I was to try to summarize the intent of the rules in one sentence, I would say that the rules try to make sure that you can't eat your cake and have it as well. The situations that you may run into most frequently are those that pertain to water hazards. Know the difference between the rules for a water hazard, marked by yellow stakes or yellow lines, and a lateral water hazard, marked by red stakes or red lines. Some of the options are the same for both and some are different. It is very important to know where you can take relief and how to drop the ball after doing so. On a number of occasions the rules can actually make things easier for you.

Let me give you some examples to emphasize the importance of knowing the rules. The 1965 U.S. Open was played at Bellerive Country Club in St. Louis. The sixth hole is a par three with the green practically surrounded by water. One of the players hit the green nicely with his tee shot and then proceeded to putt his ball off the green and into the water hazard. Evidently he did not know all the options available to him under this circumstance or was too shocked to remember them at the time. He did remember the option about taking the next shot from a spot that would keep the point where the ball last crossed the hazard between him and the hole. He crossed over to the other side of the water hazard, hit his fourth shot back to the green and two putted for a six. He did not take advantage of the option to play another ball from the same spot from which he had putted into the water. Had he done so, and with the knowledge he had gained from his first putt, he might have still made a bogey and surely not more than five.

Another example was the situation where Craig Stadler "built" a stance, when he placed a towel under his knees to protect his trousers, before playing a trouble shot from that position. This caused him to be disqualified for posting the wrong score for that hole. It was an expensive error since he was near the top of the leader board at the time. Tiger Woods, on the other hand, does know and understand the rules. In one tournament his ball ended up in the rough, where a large boulder interfered with his swing. Woods enlisted the help of several spectators, who helped him move this huge boulder. There is no way he could have done this by himself. Personally, I would like to see this rule changed. If a player is forbidden to get outside advice then I do not believe that a player should be allowed to use outside assistance to make the next stroke easier.

Finally, a player is responsible for the score on each hole as posted on the score card that he or she signs. The player is not responsible for totaling the score. If he does total them incorrectly, but the scores for each hole are correct, there is no harm done.

WHAT HAPPENS AT IMPACT?

I believe that the reader will find it interesting to learn exactly what takes place during the impact between the clubhead and the golf ball. We will consider the case of the driver that has the least amount of loft built into the face. Because of the small amount of loft on a driver, for mathematical purposes we can assume that the impact is the same as it would be for a club that has zero loft.

It has been proven through high speed photography that it takes only one-half millisecond (0.0005 seconds) from the time a stationary golf ball is first contacted by the clubhead until the ball springs clear of the club face. This may vary slightly for a thin club face, but not by very much. The backspin that is imparted to the ball, as well as any sidespin, which may cause either a hook or slice, is introduced during this brief period. Just as nothing can be done to redirect a bullet once it has left the rifle barrel, the flight of the golf ball cannot be changed by the player once it leaves the club face. You cannot steer a golf ball.

When a driver with a 205 gram clubhead, traveling at 100 miles per hour (147 feet per second), contacts a golf ball under central impact conditions (on the sweet spot with the face square), the golf ball is accelerated from zero velocity to about 212 feet per second (145 mph) in that one-half millisecond. This assumes zero face deflection. By employing two basic laws of physics, it can be shown that during this brief time the following occurs.

The golf ball is accelerated to 145 mph.

The average velocity of the combined clubhead and golf ball during impact is 81 miles per hour, equivalent to 1,426 inches per second.

During the 0.0005 second contact, the clubhead travels a mere 0.71 inches.

The clubhead speed immediately after separation is 68 mph. The theoretical value, using a perfectly elastic golf ball, would be 63 mph.

The values quoted here are based on the use of a 90 compression golf ball. Results will vary depending on the hardness of the ball and the clubhead velocity. In the case of a putter the coefficient of restitution (COR) between the ball and the putter face will be higher than when using a driver. The reason for this is that since the clubhead velocity of the putter is small, it does not compress the golf ball nearly as much as the driver does, and there will be less energy lost due to the deformation of the golf ball. When using a driver some golfers have the ability to swing the clubhead more than 100 mph, perhaps as high as 130 mph. Under these conditions, the COR will be slightly lower in value unless a higher compression ball is used. From actual test data, with a clubhead speed of 100 mph using a 90 compression ball, the COR was calculated to be 0.77.

It might be interesting to consider what would occur if the golf ball were perfectly elastic; that is, if the COR between the club and the ball was 1.00. The theoretical results using such a perfectly elastic ball, represents the ultimate performance that could be expected. Using a mechanical golf ball driving machine, 100 mph clubhead velocity, and operating in still air at sea level, a 90 compression golf ball was found to carry about 225 yards. The initial velocity of an "ideal" golf ball, one that did not compress, would be 243 fps. The carry of the of the ideal golf ball, with its COR equal to 1.00, will be in proportion to its initial velocity. At a clubhead speed of 100 mph, the ideal golf ball would then carry approximately 254 yards. While it may be possible to manufacture a golf ball with a COR greater than 0.77, the amount of improvement would be limited. We would soon reach a point where the internal stresses created would become so great that the golf ball would shatter. The golf ball must deform in an elastic manner in order to keep the internal stresses at a reasonable value. A so-called ideal golf ball with a COR equal to 1.00 might be visualized as a hollow glass sphere with the same weight and diameter as the standard golf ball. It doesn't take much imagination to know what would happen if this glass ball was struck by a driver at 100 mph, instant powdered glass.

In the case of the new thin-faced titanium drivers, a different situation is encountered. These thin-faced drivers will be discussed later. The discussion, so far, assumes a driver with a face that is rigid. This is the case for the persimmon or laminated wood drivers of the past or the stainless steel drivers with thick non-yielding faces.

This work utilizes two basic laws of physics, the Law of Conservation of Momentum and the Law of Conservation of Energy. The Law of Conservation of Momentum, as it is applied here, means that before, during, and immediately following impact, the total amount of momentum in the system remains unchanged. The use of the Law of Conservation of Energy is somewhat more complicated, since work is done on the ball when it is first compressed and then, again, when it expands to return to its original spherical shape. The Coefficient of Resolution (COR) represents the energy remaining after the ball returns to its original spherical shape. If we had used a spherical piece of modeling clay instead of the usual golf ball, the clay would stick to the clubhead after impact, in which case the COR would be zero. However, if the weight of the clay is the same as the weight of a golf ball, the velocity of the clubhead and the attached clay would be the same as the average for the clubhead and a real golf ball.

Again, all of the foregoing was based on an impact situation in which the club face has little loft, such as a driver, and where the club face is perpendicular to the swing path at impact. If the face of the club is open or closed at impact, or if the path of the clubhead is not perpendicular to the face alignment due to some swing imperfection, side spin is introduced. This, too, is a waste of energy and it will result in still further loss of distance as well as a ball path which is off the target line.

What happens in that half millisecond of a direct central contact between a golf ball and the club face that does have loft? Since every club face does have some loft built into it, backspin is created, the amount of backspin depending on the degree of loft; the greater the loft of the clubhead, the greater will be the angular velocity (backspin) of the golf ball. The ball will flatten most on the face of the driver that has the least amount of loft. In order to increase the length of a drive by getting more roll at the end of the carry, many golfers use a higher tee and play the ball farther forward in their stance. This makes it possible to strike the ball after the clubhead has started to move up. In this case less backspin will be created and this will result in more roll after the ball lands on the fairway. Some golfers who utilize this method use wood tees three or more inches long. Chi Chi Rodriguez did this.

When stronger golfers began to use titanium drivers fabricated with thin faces, it was reported that they were hitting the ball farther than they did with rigid-faced drivers. Thus, the term "trampoline effect" came into being. At first sight this would seem to defy the laws of physics. With a rigid-faced driver only the golf ball is deformed and all of the lost energy is contributed to the ball. This amounted to a loss of energy equal to about twenty-three percent using a 90 compression ball. With the new driver we have a club face thin enough to deflect, and at first glance it would seem that we should lose even more energy since now both the ball and the club face deform. However, since the face does deflect, the ball will not deform as much as it does with a driver that has a rigid face. It follows then, that the additional energy retained by the ball exceeds the loss of energy due to club face deflection. Consequently, the coefficient of restitution for the ball and the thin-faced driver combination is higher than that of the ball and a driver with a rigid face. In that case we need not throw away the old laws of physics. Claims for the new COR run in a range of 0.83 to 0.86.

For those who are curious and/or mathematically inclined, the calculations for the material presented in this chapter will be found in Appendix Two.

THE SHAPE OF THE GOLF SHOT

The nature and shape of the golf shot is determined over a very short period of time. As mentioned in the previous chapter, when using a driver, the ball is in contact with the face for one-half millisecond (0.0005 seconds), during which time the clubhead travels approximately three-quarters of an inch. After the ball leaves the club face, it acts no differently than any other free missile, whether it be a javelin, the pebble from a sling shot, or the bullet from a gun. Its behavior is the result of what has occurred prior to release. The only external influences that can affect its flight are gravity, wind, and atmospheric conditions, namely temperature and barometric pressure. If we assume zero wind, then during a single golf stroke all external influences remain constant and need not be considered in this discussion. The shape of the shot, or trajectory, is determined by the following factors:

- markings of the golf ball cover
- golf ball velocity
- launch angle
- backspin
- sidespin (clockwise or counter-clockwise)

This discussion will be limited to the trajectory of a golf ball impacted by a driver. Again, the driver has so little loft that the physics involved can be assumed to be the same as if impact occurred using a club with zero loft, a central impact condition.

THE GOLF BALL

Dimple depth and dimple pattern, particularly the former, are important factors because they affect the amount of lift that is developed by the golf ball, curvature in flight to either side, and the stability of the golf ball's flight path. The barrel of a gun has rifling for the same purpose, to stabilize the path of the bullet. Without dimples or markings, the flight of the golf ball would be unpredictable. As mentioned elsewhere, using a driver, a smooth golf ball might not carry 100 yards, even when struck by touring professionals.

When the Haskell wound rubber ball was introduced, about 1900, it was nick-named the "Bounding Billy." The ball was a huge improvement over the solid gutta percha ball because unlike its predecessor, it would bounce and roll after striking the ground. I had a few gutta percha balls in my collection and I tried hitting one of them. It was an unpleasant feeling. It felt as if I had hit a billiard ball. The sensation might not have been as bad had I hit the guttie using a wood-shafted golf club. A wood shaft will absorb vibration much better than does a steel shaft. For many years the dimples on most golf balls were uniform in size and arranged in a concentric circular pattern. Tests on golf balls were performed in Great Britain during the 1960s by the Golf Society of Great Britain. Their test results showed that the optimum dimple depth was 0.010 inches. When the dimples were not as deep, the ball did not develop as much lift and it did not carry as far. When the dimple patter exceeded 0.010 inches, the lift did not improve any further and there was an increase in aerodynamic drag. For both of these reasons the ball did not carry as far. In these tests a ball with dimples that were only 0.002 inches deep carried half as far as the ball with dimples that were 0.010 inches deep.

The matter of initial golf ball velocity is a function of the player's strength and the efficiency with which he swings the club. The elements that affect the initial velocity of the golf ball are the clubhead speed, the coefficient of restitution between the ball and the clubhead, and the weight of the clubhead. For these discussions the standard golf ball as approved by the USGA and the R&A will be used. Once the matter of the weight of both the golf ball and clubhead has been established, it appears that a linear relationship exists between the length of carry and the clubhead speed at impact.

LAUNCH ANGLE

The launch angle—the angle between the initial golf ball path and the horizontal—is affected by two factors. These are the loft of the club face and the path of the clubhead at the instant that impact occurs. Assume that the face of the club is perpendicular to the line of flight at impact. The term, "path," refers to whether the ball is struck a descending blow, is contacted at the bottom of the swing, or is struck an ascending blow. This affects not only the effective loft of the clubhead at impact but also the amount of backspin that is imparted to the ball.

Drivers are manufactured with various loft angles to accommodate the different swings of golfers. Even when the ball is struck at the very bottom of the downswing, the launch angle is not the same as the loft of the club face. Since the clubhead is moving forward at the time of impact, the launch angle will be the result of both the loft of the clubhead and the velocity of the clubhead. Velocity, unlike speed, is a vector quantity. This means that it is composed of both speed and direction. Speed is a scalar quantity; it has magnitude but not direction. The launch angle of the ball will be less than the loft angle of the golf club. After impact, the flight path will, at first, be steeper as a result of the lift created by the backspin. When hitting into the wind, the effective velocity, which affects lift, is the sum of the initial golf ball velocity due to impact plus the velocity of the head wind. This can increase the amount of lift by a considerable amount. With more lift the ball will climb higher than it would in the absence of a headwind. The converse is true with a trailing wind; the flight path will be lower. Therefore, after striking the ground, the ball will roll less when hitting into the wind and it will roll farther when hitting with the wind.

If the club face is perpendicular to the path of the clubhead and the ball is struck on the sweetspot, the flight of the ball will be straight. In such cases pure backspin is the only rotation imparted to the golf ball. If this impact condition is not met, curvature is introduced to the flight pattern of the golf ball. A draw or fade will result when the club face is square to the target line but the path of the clubhead is either inside-out or outside-in when the ball is struck at or near the center of percussion, or the sweetspot. If the swing path is outside-in and the face is open, the ball may start left and then curve sharply to the right, the dreaded slice results. A smothered hook will occur when the path is outside–in combined with a closed club face. There are a great many ways of striking a golf ball that will cause a curved flight pattern. The ones that have been discussed so far are a result of misalignment of the swing plane or the face of the clubhead, which cause sidespin. Better golfers can do this intentionally and use these golf shots as tools.

BACKSPIN AND SIDESPIN—THE GEAR EFFECT

It is good to remember that unless some external force is applied, nothing can change the shape of the golf shot after the ball leaves the face of the club. This conforms to Newton's First Law and there are no exceptions. It should also be borne in mind that the center of percussion may not be located at the center of the club face. One must be careful not to make this erroneous assumption when trying to establish the contact points for straight center hits. The ball only goes straight when struck on the center of percussion with a properly aligned face and clubhead path.

The term "gear effect" was introduced in an earlier chapter with regard to the kind of putter that has its center of gravity an appreciable distance behind the putter face. At this point we will look into the term as it applies to the other clubs in the golf bag. What follows here will explain why drivers and fairway woods have curved faces.

Gear effect is a phenomenon which is due to off-center contact between the club face and the golf ball. When present, gear effect causes a golf ball that has been contacted off the center of the club face to spin in such a way as to curve back in the opposite direction from which it was initially deflected. Some people believe that gear effect is the result of the bulge (convex curvature) built into the face of drivers and fairway clubs. As the reader will see, bulge is built in the face of the driver to compensate for too much gear effect.

On an off-center hit, the club face will either open or close depending on whether the contact occurs toward the toe or the heel. When there is an off-center impact the clubhead will rotate about its center of gravity (c.g.). For example, in the case of a toe hit by a right-handed golfer, the clubhead will rotate clockwise. Where the c.g. is well behind the face, as in the case of a driver or fairway wood, the contact point on the club face will not only move back, but it will also swing to the right across the back of the ball, which is partly flat at that point. Under these conditions the interaction of between the club face and the ball is similar to the action that takes place between two meshed gears, hence the term *gear effect*. As the clubhead turns in one direction the ball will rotate in the opposite direction. When the face of the clubhead opens, due to the off-center contact toward the toe of the clubhead, a counter clockwise spin is imparted to the ball. Again, the amount of gear effect depends on the distance the c.g. is located behind the club face and the shape of the club face. In the case of an iron, due to its relatively thin head, the c.g. of the clubhead is near the face and the gear effect, if any, will be so small that it will not be noticeable. For a driver or fairway club, because of its shape, the gear effect is significant.

If the club face of a driver is perfectly flat, the gear effect would not merely reduce the fade spin caused by the opening of the club face; it would do much more. This could cause severe right to left curvature of the golf ball flight from toe hits and the opposite from heel hits. In order to compensate for excessive gear effect, drivers and fairway woods are designed with face curvature, called bulge. The amount of bulge required is dictated by the distance that the c.g. lies behind the club face. The bulge is usually the arc of a circle with the radius of curvature anywhere from eight to fourteen inches. Think of the bulge as being your helper for excessive gear effect. Persimmon and laminated maple clubheads have the center of gravity well behind the club face and require a considerable amount of face curvature to counteract excessive gear effect. Earlier stainless steel metal woods had the center of gravity closer to the club face and required less bulge. In fact some metal woods were built with too much bulge for the center of gravity location and as a result, on a toe hit, the ball started too far off line to the right for the gear effect to be able to bring the ball back to the fairway. Titanium is the club designer's dream metal because it has such a large strength-to-weight ratio. Consequently, thin shell drivers with volumes as large as 450 cubic centimeters can be built, and because of the light weight of titanium it is still possible to distribute additional weight to strategic locations in the club-head. The additional weight can be added internally or externally to control the final weight and center of gravity location.

For a driver head weighing 205 grams, it has been determined that during direct impact the average force applied to the face of a driver traveling at 100 miles per hour is nearly 1500 pounds. This means that the peak force must be close to 2000 pounds. When using rigid stainless steel, the face of the driver had to have a thickness of approximately 0.125 inches in order to withstand this enormous force. When some of the stronger players develop a clubhead speed near 130 miles per hour, the impact force increases by as much as 30 percent. In order to keep the completed clubhead within acceptable weight limits it was essential that the rest of the shell that goes to make up the clubhead be extremely thin, as thin as 0.030 inches. With so much weight being concentrated in the club face, the center of gravity of the large stainless steel clubhead was fairly close to the club face. When designed correctly, these clubs were built with a small amount of bulge; that is, with a larger radius of curvature.

In the case of a clubhead with a thin face made of titanium, the fact that the face deflects at impact reduces the amount of stress experienced by the face during impact. This leads to what is commonly referred to as trampoline effect, which was mentioned elsewhere.

The title of this chapter is "The Shape of the Golf Shot." This subject must include air, the medium through which the golf ball travels. It is interesting to note how much the air can vary from one place to another and from one time to another at the same place.

The effect of humidity on the flight of a golf ball is often highly exaggerated. Humidity actually makes the air lighter, but never as much as one percent. I have heard television announcers, as well as tour players, comment to the effect that the players have to adjust when playing in Florida after playing in the western desert due to the humidity. On other occasions I have overheard the statement to the effect that "because of the high humidity the ball isn't going as far." This is not the case. In the first place, the dry air of the desert is heavier, if anything, than the more humid air encountered in Florida, at the same temperature, but not enough to make a real difference to a golfer.

This is not difficult to understand when you realize that clouds which are composed of water vapor float at altitudes where the air is lighter. This can only mean that clouds, like the moisture in the air that causes humidity, are made up of water vapor and that water vapor is lighter than dry air. Further, the temperatures in Florida and the western desert are not much different from each other, except during the morning. The air may be cooler in the desert during the early morning and the ball will not travel as far. I believe the remarks I referred to above fit into the adage, "The eyes see only what they look for and what they look for is already in the mind." The only factor that does affect the golf ball in flight is air density. Let us look into that and forget humidity.

The two primary factors that affect air density are pressure and temperature. These will be discussed separately and then various combinations of these factors will be used to determine the combined effect. During this discussion relative air density will be expressed as a ratio, the ratio of the actual air density to the density of "standard sea level air." By international agreement, "standard sea level air is air at a temperature of 59 degrees Fahrenheit

(15 degrees Celsius) and a pressure of 2116 pound per square foot, equivalent to a barometric reading of 29.92 inches of mercury). In equation form:

Density Ratio = (p/po) x (To/T)
Where: p = actual air pressure
         p_o = 29.92 inches of mercury or 2116 lbs./sq.ft.
         T = absolute temperature = 460 + temp. in deg. F.
         T_o = absolute temperature at sea level = 519 deg. F.

The density of standard sea level air = 0.002378 slugs per cubic foot, which is the equivalent of a weight of 0.0765 pounds per cubic foot. (Why would anyone choose the term slugs?) You will note from the density ratio equation that air density is proportional to the air pressure and inversely proportional to the absolute temperature. Absolute zero is the temperature where molecular activity ceases. Over the range of temperatures that golf is played, the temperature variation from one place to the next or one time to the next is not likely to be more than 50 degrees on the Fahrenheit scale. Therefore, the maximum effect of temperature on density will rarely exceed ten percent.

Air pressure, however, is a major factor. There are two reasons for changes in air pressure. The greatest change is that caused by a change in altitude. In Standard Air, pressure decreases more than three percent for each 1000 feet in altitude. For example, the air pressure at 6,000 feet is approximately 80 percent of the air pressure at sea level. At 10,000 thousand feet it is about 70 percent of the sea level value. For simplicity we refer to altitude as a reference for air pressure.

The other change in barometric pressure is caused by normal weather movements. Most of us are aware that the barometric pressure goes down as a storm approaches and goes up as fair weather approaches. However, we seldom experience changes in air pressure due to highs and lows of more than 0.2 inches of mercury from the standard pressure for any particular altitude. Since this represents only about one-half of one percent it can be disregarded, for all practical purposes.

The lift force caused by backspin and the aerodynamic drag of the golf ball are both directly proportional to air density. Therefore, as altitude increases the ball will not climb as high, but it will go farther due to the decrease in aerodynamic drag. On the plus side, due to the lower density, the golf ball will not hook or slice as much at higher altitudes.

Golf ball drag is an interesting subject. Normally we think of aerodynamic drag as a function of the shape of the object, such as a blunt shape compared to a streamlined shape. Drag due to shape and skin friction is referred to as parasite drag. Shape drag applies to the golf ball. However, it is only part of the story because there is another factor, which is the result of the backspin that creates a lifting force. The golf ball, like an airplane, experiences two types of drag, the parasite drag, already mentioned, and an induced drag component. The induced drag is caused (induced) by the lift that results from backspin. For a golf ball the induced drag is appreciable. The induced drag of an airplane varies inversely with the square of the wing span. Therefore, slower-flying (sailplanes for example) and long-range aircraft are designed with wings that have high aspect ratios in order to minimize the induced drag. Since the golf ball flight falls in the low aspect ratio category, (equal to 1.0), induced drag is a factor about which nothing can be done.

As mentioned earlier, the temperature of the golf ball can affect its initial velocity and therefore the carry because it affects the elasticity (coefficient of restitution) of the ball. A warm ball will carry farther than one that is cold. A decrease in temperature of 40 degrees F. can result in a loss of 15 yards on a 200-yard drive. Remember this when you are playing under cold conditions. A wise player will start with warm golf balls and keep a few balls in his pocket for body heat. Then he can change to a warm ball after each hole. This is a different problem from the effect of ambient air temperature as discussed above.

On a lighter note, when I lived in Morgantown, West Virginia, I told one of the members of our club about this. During the cold season, he would heat his rubber wound golf balls in his kitchen oven before going out to play. One day he forgot about them being in the oven and the balls exploded. This left a terrible mess of both latex and the fluid from the liquid center adhering to the walls of the oven. It nearly resulted in a divorce. It is difficult to quantify the exact amount of extra distance that would be obtained with each club as a result of a lowering in air density. It will vary with the class of golfer and the type of golf ball used.

Getting back to what was stated when this subject was introduced, the only reason that a ball might go farther in the western desert than in Florida might be if that desert location was at a higher altitude. The highest desert course that has been played on the PGA Tour is at Tucson, Arizona, where the elevation is approximately 2400 feet. Desert courses are played during the winter when the temperatures are relatively cool in the morning. The air density in Tucson at that time of the year will probably be about seven percent less than in Florida. At Phoenix or the California deserts there will be little difference, if any.

Playing at the elevation of Colorado Springs is a different story. I played at Colorado Springs when the temperature was 90° F. Therefore the air density was 25 percent lower than under standard sea level conditions. A player who normally hits a drive 200 yards at sea level would probably hit the golf ball 230 yards under these conditions.

I am sure that most all of you either witnessed or heard about the time that Alan Shepard hit a six iron shot on the moon. Since there isn't any air on the moon, his golf ball didn't have any drag, but neither did it develop any lift. The cover markings did not help on the moon. It was a good thing that he used an iron with about 35 degrees loft. The only force that acted on his golf ball after it left the club face was the force of the moon's gravity, which is one sixth that of the gravitational force here on the planet Earth. Then again, on the moon his golf ball weighed but little more than one-quarter of an ounce.

To anyone that might be thinking of building a golf course on the moon, I would suggest that you take into consideration that daytime temperatures are in the order of 212 degrees F. and night time temperatures drop to a minus 345 degrees F.

The table below shows the density ratio vs. elevations, on Earth, up to 10,000 feet elevation under standard air conditions and at a temperature of 85 degrees F. Note that at 10,000 feet and a temperature of 85 degrees the air is 35 percent lighter than it is at sea level at the same temperature.

TABLE 1 AIR DENSITY RATIO								
Altitude (feet)	Pressure	Temp. Deg. F.	Temp. Abso-lute Deg. R.	p/p_o	T_o/T	T_o/T_{85}	Density Ratio Std. Air	Density Ratio 85 deg.
0	29.92	59.0	518.0	1.000	1.000	0.952	1.000	0.952
1000	28.86	55.4	514.4	0.965	1.007	0.952	0.971	0.918
2000	27.82	51.9	510.9	0.930	1.014	0.952	0.943	0.885
3000	26.82	48.3	507.3	0.896	1.021	0.952	0.915	0.854
4000	25.84	44.7	503.7	0.864	1.028	0.952	0.888	0.822
5000	24.89	41.2	500.2	0.832	1.036	0.952	0.861	0.792
6000	23.98	37.6	496.6	0.801	10.43	0.952	0.836	0.763
7000	23.09	34.0	493.0	0.772	1.051	0.952	0.811	0.735
8000	22.22	30.5	489.5	0.743	1.058	0.952	0.786	0.707
9000	21.38	26.9	485.9	0.715	1.066	0.952	0.762	0.680
10000	20.57	23.3	482.3	0.688	1.074	0.952	0.738	0.655

MOMENT OF INERTIA

This chapter will deal with the term, *moment of inertia* in more depth. It isn't as technical as it sounds. It is true that if a person wants to calculate the moment of inertia of some irregular object then that person would need to have knowledge of integral calculus. In most cases this has been done for us and values of moment of inertia for different areas and solids can be found in handbooks. My reason for going into this is to give the golfer a feel for how moment of inertia can affect a golf club at impact, and secondly how it affects the feel of a golf club swung by a golfer.

What may cause problems for some people is the fact that there are different types of moment of inertia as they apply to golf. In general we deal with some type of moment of inertia in every day life, perhaps without realizing it. The different types of moment of inertia are:

- Area moment of inertia
- Mass moment of inertia
- Polar moment of inertia

The dictionary definition for moment of inertia does not tell the layman very much. My dictionary defines it as: "the sum of the products of the mass and the square of the perpendicular distance to the axis of rotation of each particle in a body rotating about an axis."

Actually, the moment of inertia of an object represents a measure of the ability of that object to resist bending, or angular acceleration or torsion. The cross-sectional shape and cross section area of a golf club shaft determines the stiffness of that shaft. It also determines the ability of the shaft to resist torsion. This torsion is often referred to as torque. The term torque in this sense is a misnomer because torque really refers to what is being applied. The distribution of weight in the head of every club in your bag determines its resistance to deflection on off-center impacts. The moment of inertia of the golf club as a whole determines the feel of the club while it is being swung and will affect the clubhead speed that that a golfer can attain.

Moving to the golf club situation, many of you have no doubt seen golf clubs advertised as having a "larger sweetspot." This term is used a great deal by the manufacturers of putters and irons that have perimeter weighting. The term "larger sweetspot" was also used as the transition was made from drivers and fairway clubs made of wood to those made of metal. At that time, all the metal clubs in that classification were made of stainless steel. When metal woods were introduced, players felt that these new clubs hit the ball straighter than those made of persimmon or laminated maple wood. What actually took place was that the new metal woods were inherently perimeter weighted (greater moment of inertia) and therefore more forgiving on off-center hits.

What is the sweetspot? In terms of physics, the sweetspot is the center of percussion. The actual size of the sweetspot is a point the size of the pointed end of a needle. If a golf club contacts the ball so that the center of the ball is in line with the center of percussion there will be no angular deflection of the club face and the ball will carry farther and straighter than if contacted any other place on the face of the club. The technical definition of the center of percussion is: "That point in a body, free to move about a fixed axis, at which the body may be struck fairly without jarring the axis." In the case of the clubhead, the axis is the center of gravity of the clubhead. It should be pointed out that a line through the center of percussion does not necessarily pass through the center of gravity. In the case of the clubhead it does come pretty close to doing so.

As mentioned above the definition of the center of percussion refers to a point. In dealing with the impact between a golf ball and the face of a club, it is not reasonable to think of a golf ball striking a point, the center of percussion, because during impact the ball flattens on the face of the clubhead and has a circular footprint which may be close to an inch in diameter. The size of the footprint made by the ball will vary depending on the hardness of the ball and the clubhead speed. Consequently, even on an off-center hit, the part of the ball that is flattened during impact will almost always cover the center of percussion. During a perfect contact situation, the center of percussion is at the center of the contact area. Even the slightest deviation from this ideal condition will result in some angular rotation of the face and cause side spin.

In the case of perfect hits with a driver, neither the size nor shape of the clubhead will make any difference in the result if the weight of the clubhead and the velocity of the clubhead are identical. This statement does not apply to the newer, thin-faced large volume titanium drivers.

What then is meant by the expression "larger sweetspot"? This characteristic refers to a clubhead that is more forgiving on off-center hits, a clubhead that has greater resistance to opening or closing (rotating) on off-center impacts. This characteristic is what we referred to as moment of inertia (MOI) Note that the definition of moment of inertia refers to the square of its distance from the axis. In mathematical terms this means that moment of inertia is a *second* moment.

In the case of the clubhead, the axis referred to above passes through the center of gravity (c.g.) because it is about the c.g. that the clubhead will rotate on off-center hits. Since the moment of inertia is proportional to the square of the distance of the mass elements from the c.g., substantial increases in moment of inertia can be achieved by distributing the weight in such a manner as to favor the heel and toe in the case of irons (cavity back) and the perimeter of the clubhead in the case of hollow metal drivers and fairway woods.

Let us look at some common examples of things that are familiar to all of us in order to get a better feel for the term moment of inertia, how it works and how it is used. We have already mentioned the case of a diver, gymnast, or an acrobat. When any of them want to perform multiple somersaults, these athletes will bend their knees and grab their ankles, bringing their extremities (the arms and legs) closer to the center of gravity. This reduces the moment of inertia to such an extent that they are able to do as many as three somersaults where they might be able to do only one in the extended position.

The other example was that of the figure skater who spins at a high rate of speed on the tips of the skates. In order to accomplish this feat, the skater will hug himself or herself with both arms, thereby reducing the moment of inertia about the vertical spinning axis. The skater is able to reduce the rate of spin by extending both arms out to the sides. This increases the skater's moment of inertia appreciably.

Both of the above cases represent dynamic situations. In a static situation let us take the case of a two-by-eight wood board that might be used as a joist to support the floor in a house. This board has a cross-section area equal to sixteen square inches. You will always see these joists installed standing on end with the two-inch dimension at the top and bottom. The reason for this is that the moment of inertia of the board is sixteen (16) times greater when it is standing on end than it would be if the eight inch sides were at the top and bottom. This is now understandable since, by definition, moment of inertia is proportional to the square of the distance of the mass elements from the axis. The moment of inertia for a rectangular beam is:

$$MOI = bh^3/12$$

Where b and h are the dimensions of the base and height.

When the eight-inch side of the board is horizontal, b=8 and h=2 and

$$MOI = 8 \times 2^3 = 8 \times 8 = 64.$$

When the two-inch side of the board is horizontal, b=2 and h=8 and

MOI = 2 x 8^3 = 2 x 512 = 1024.

The second MOI is sixteen times greater than the first example. This is an everyday example of area moment of inertia. The farther the mass or area is from the neutral axis—usually the centroid or center of gravity—the larger will be the value of MOI. When steel is used in the construction of a building, the steel will usually be in the form of "I" beams. The "I" beam has most of its mass in the top and bottom flanges. This helps not only to make the beam stronger but also lighter and less expensive.

Next, let us take the case of a sphere, which is not very much different from the shape of a high volume driver. The moment of inertia of a solid sphere about an axis through its center of gravity is:

MOI = $2/5Mr^2$ where M is the mass and r is the radius of the sphere.

In the case of a hollow, thin-walled sphere:

MOI = Mr^2

The solid sphere can be compared to a driver with a head made of solid wood, where the hollow sphere is analogous to a thin-walled metal driver. If the spheres have identical weights and radii, the MOI of the hollow sphere would be two and one half (2-1/2) times that of the solid sphere. To the golfer this means that the hollow metal driver is much more effective in resisting angular deflection from off-center hits than a driver made of solid material.

Now let us look at a putter design. This is a prime example of the benefit that can be derived from heel and toe weighting: that results in a greater moment of inertia. Assume that we have a putter made from solid square bar stock. The dimensions of the head, in inches, are 4 x 1 x 1, and the volume is 4 cubic inches. Since we are looking for numbers on which to base a comparison, we will assume unit mass per unit volume. The MOI of this putter head about an axis perpendicular to the top of the putter passing through the center of gravity calculates to be 5.67. This putter and the axis used for calculating this moment of inertia is shown in Figure 1. Figure 2 shows a second putter where elements A and B have been moved from their central location and placed behind the putter at each end. The moment of inertia of Putter No. 2 about the same axis location is 8.54 an increase of 51 percent. The weight of the putter has not changed yet the MOI has increased to 8.54. Figure 3 shows a third putter where elements A and B have been moved to positions farther from the axis, increasing its length to five inches. Again, the weight of the putter is unchanged. The MOI of the putter in Figure 3 calculates to be 10.42. This is an increase of 84 percent over putter No.1 and 21 percent over putter No.2.

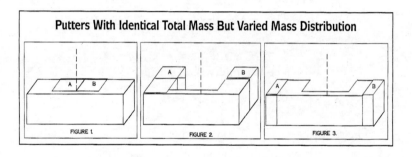

Putters With Identical Total Mass But Varied Mass Distribution

FIGURE 1.   FIGURE 2.   FIGURE 3.

TABLE 2
MOMENT OF INERTIA FOR THREE PUTTERS

Putter Number	Moment of Inertia	Percent Increase Over Putter No. 1
1	5.668	----------------
2	8.542	51
3	10.417	84

THE FEEL OF THE GOLF CLUB

The term moment of inertia has now been used in several places in this book. Each of those times the term was used with respect to the clubhead and the effect of moment of inertia on off-center impacts.

The moment of inertia of the golf club as a whole is also an important consideration. It is a major factor that limits the club-head speed that a player can develop. Initial golf ball velocity and the resulting distance is a direct function of clubhead speed. Some of the readers have probably used "warm up clubs" or have tried to swing two clubs at a time before starting a round of golf in order to loosen up. Those who have done this know that a warm up club cannot be swung as fast as a single golf club. The reason for this is the larger moment of inertia of the practice club or clubs. Some years ago there was a heavy warm up club, with a Gene Sara-zen autograph, sold on the retail market. Other warm up devices include a donut-shaped weight that can be slipped down near the head of a wood, and weighted head covers. Factors that directly affect the moment of inertia of a golf club are the clubhead weight, shaft weight, and shaft length. Since the grip at the top of the shaft is under the hands it contributes so little to the total moment of inertia that it may be ignored. Shaft length and head weight have the greatest effect on overall moment of inertia.

Some mathematical equations are included in this chapter as backup for several of these statements. Readers can skip the mathematical equations without losing any of the continuity.

With the advent of graphite shafts there was a tendency to use a longer shaft and/or heavier clubheads. Evidently, there is the belief that since graphite shafts are considerably lighter than those made of steel, a longer shaft will result in additional clubhead speed and therefore added distance. In some cases this may be partially true, but it will affect your accuracy. First, it is more difficult to square up the club face at the end of a longer shaft because the player's arms cannot be lengthened to match the additional shaft length. Secondly, a longer shaft will usually require that the player exert more effort than he or she would normally use, in which case we are not dealing with equal inputs. We already know that in general, moment of inertia represents the property of an object to resist any change in angular velocity.

For example, it is much easier to start to spin a bicycle wheel and tire on its axle than a truck wheel and tire. By the same token it is much more difficult to stop a truck tire and wheel that is rotating than it is a bicycle wheel and tire. The reason for this is that a truck wheel and tire has a much greater moment of inertia and, therefore, offers more resistance to any change in its motion. Let's repeat the definition of MOI:

> Moment of inertia is the sum of the products of the mass and
> the *square* of the perpendicular distance to the axis of rotation
> for each particle rotating about that axis.

This is a technical definition, to be sure. It is included here, again, in order to point out that the definition of moment of inertia includes the word "square" and this is what makes moment of inertia a second moment rather than a first moment, as in the case of the swingweight of a golf club.

If we apply this same definition to the golf club as a whole, we must consider all three components that go to make up the golf club: the clubhead, the shaft, and the grip. As for the axis of rotation, it is generally accepted that the axis passes through a point four to five inches from the butt end of the club, just below the top hand on the grip. This is important to the golfer because the speed of the clubhead at impact, and therefore the distance that will be achieved is related to the moment of inertia of the club as a whole. For the same physical effort, as the moment of inertia of the club is increased, the acceleration of the clubhead that can be achieved on the downswing decreases. The moment of inertia of the golf club is not really a factor during the backswing, since the purpose of the backswing is merely to place the clubhead in the proper position at the top. A study of the backswings of the best PGA Tour players will reveal a considerable difference in the amount of time required to get the clubhead to the point at the top where the direction is reversed. For the less talented player, the slower the backswing, the better is that player's chance of getting things in order for a good, accelerating downswing.

Considering a complete golf club, the clubhead is by far the heaviest component, followed by the shaft and then the grip. Further, the particles of mass that go to make up the head are the farthest from the axis, those of the shaft are next, while those of the grip are quite close to the axis mentioned above. In order to provide a rough idea of the contribution of each part of the club to the moment of inertia of the club as a whole, consider the case of a driver with a 205 gram head and a 90 gram shaft.

TABLE 3 CONTRIBUTION OF COMPONENTS TO TOTAL MOMENT OF INERTIA				
	M = Mass (Oz.)	R = Radius of Gyration (inches)	MR^2	Percent of Moment of Inertia
Head	7.05	39.0	10723	87
Shaft	3.17	22.5	1604	13
Grip	1.87	5.0	47	0

Throughout this chapter we will deal only with the moment of inertia of the complete golf club. It is this moment of inertia that the player senses when he or she swings the golf club. It also the determining factor in how fast the player can swing the clubhead. In order to simplify the calculations, an approximate method of determining the value of the moment of inertia is employed here. For example, since the contribution of the grip to the total Moment of Inertia is less than one-half of one percent, it was assigned a value of zero in Table 3. Therefore we will only be concerned with the contributions of the clubhead and the shaft. Mathematically, the moment of inertia of any object is expressed by the mass times the square of the radius of gyration. The radius of gyration is a mathematical term which simply represents the distance from the axis to a point where, if the entire mass was concentrated there, its moment of inertia would be the same. For the purposes of simplification, the following assumptions are made:

The shaft is a thin circular cylinder.

The weight of the head, M, is assumed to be concentrated at a point one inch above the sole.

Based on these assumptions the moment of inertia of the shaft is:

$$I_{shaft} = m[(1-5)/12]^2 / 3$$

where: m = the weight of the shaft

1 = length of the shaft in inches

As usual the whole is the sum of the parts, therefore

$$I = I_{head} + I_{shaft}$$

$$I = M[(1-5)/12]^2 + m[\{1-5)/12]^2 /3$$

M is the weight of the clubhead

$$I = [(1-5)/12]^2(M+m/3)$$

The reason for showing the above equation is that an examination of the term in the bracket $(M + m)/3$ reveals the relative size of the contributions made by the head and the shaft to the total moment of inertia. Table 4 shows these values for a range of shafts that are currently available for use.

TABLE 4
HOW SHAFT WEIGHT AFFECTS
MOMENT OF INERTIA (MOM)

Shaft Weight (grams)	Head Contribution To MOM (percent)	Shaft Contribution To MOM (percent)	Reduction Of MOM (percent)
120	83.4	16.6	0
90	86.9	13.1	4.1
60	90.8	9.2	8.2

The following example shows the moment of inertia calculations for a typical metal wood with a 200 gram clubhead. It is included in order to provide a numerical value for a typical driver configuration.

M = 200 grams = 0.441 lbs.

m = 90 grams = 0.198 lbs.

(1-5) = 44–5 = 39 in (3.25) ft.

$I = (3.25)^2 (0.441+0.198/3) = 5.35$ lb.ft.^{2}

Based on this simplified equation for Moment of Inertia, it becomes quite easy to determine the effect of changing shaft weights and/or head weights on the overall Moment of Inertia.

From Table 4 it can be seen that changing to a lighter weight shaft would decrease the value of the Moment of Inertia by a significant amount. Therefore the player could get more clubhead speed (and distance) by replacing the steel shaft with a graphite shaft and swinging the clubhead faster. In many cases the mistake is made of increasing the clubhead weight when using a graphite shaft. This is done in order to bring the swingweight back to some magical value, say D-1. Adding weight to the head in this manner could be counter productive, because the moment of inertia will now be greater than the original club with the steel shaft and the player might actually lose clubhead speed and distance. When, instead, the swingweight is brought back to the magic number by adding length to the shaft, the moment of inertia is still increased and the club may be a little more difficult to control in addition to not being able to swing it as fast.

A player who is accustomed to swing his old D-1 golf club at a certain speed may continue to swing the new graphite-shafted club, which has a smaller moment of inertia at the same speed, not realizing that the club can now be swung faster. Habits are not easy to break. Tour professionals and many others know how to make controlled swings using almost all of the muscular effort they possess. Some can generate clubhead speeds as high as 130 miles per hour using a standard weight driver.

Moment of inertia in the sense that it is used in this chapter is a matter that has been neglected for too long by the golf industry. The idea that all men's clubs should be in the D-0 to D-2 swingweight range with a driver of 43 inches, (now 44 inches), has no real foundation. During the "low tech" era, golf clubs were designed according to some club maker's feel. A woman's club in the C-3 to C-5 range could be using the same head as a man's club. The difference in club length reduces the swing weight from D-1 to something close to a C-5.

When a man chokes down one-half inch on the grip, for all practical purposes he is swinging a woman's club, except for the shaft stiffness. It doesn't seem reasonable to think that a 5'2" woman weighing 100 pounds can swing a golf club in the same manner as a 6 foot, 185 pound man. This is where the overall moment of inertia of the golf club enters into the equation and should be taken into account.

It is quite likely that the player would lose some of the feel of the club if the head were made appreciably lighter while still using a steel shaft that weighs 120 grams. Composite shafts are now available that weigh less than one-half as much as steel shafts, yet golf clubs are still manufactured to the same old swingweight standard. Swingweight balances were originally created for the purpose of matching the clubs in a set, not for an alpha numeric value. It is a poor way to match clubs in a set. Yet, it has persevered for more than sixty years.

Now we will deal with setting a value for the overall moment of inertia and matching golf clubs to a constant value of moment of inertia rather than by constant swingweight.

There is no accepted standard for the length of clubs or for the loft of a clubhead. Until about twenty years before this book was written, most clubs were built the same way by most of the manufacturers. Irons were built so that the clubs varied by one-half inch from one club to its neighbor, with the five iron being 37 inches long. The five iron had 30 degree loft and there was a four degree difference between clubs.

When graphite shafts came into use, competition increased, not only from new companies in the United States, but from Japan, as well. To make their clubs seem to be superior, some manufacturers put less loft on the club and added one-half inch in length. The number on the club remained the same. The player was fooled into thinking that these irons hit the ball farther. In fact, however, the golfer was hitting a club that was marked as a five iron, when it was actually the same as a four iron in the set of clubs that was being replaced. The golfer never knew the difference. What has happened is that sets of irons no longer included a two iron.

MATCHING GOLF CLUBS:
THE WAY IT IS DONE

It has surprised me that during the past sixty to seventy years that there has been no progress made in the golf club industry with regard to matching golf clubs in a set or determining the optimum weight for clubheads.

According to early reports, the first system for matching golf clubs was to have a set for which each club's head weight times the length of the club was equal to a constant. This method was replaced by the Lorythmic Scale with its arbitrary alpha-numeric scale readings, credited to an engineer named Robert Adams during the mid 1930s. The Lorythmic Scale, and later the Official Scale and the Prorythmic Scale, were marketed by Kenneth Smith. The only difference between the Lorythmic and Prorythmic Scale was that the latter can also measure the dead weight of the golf club. Swingweight and dead weight are non-related functions. The Prorythmic Scale merely did away with the necessity for separate devices.

Kenneth Smith obtained a patent for the Official Scale in 1952. This device used a twelve-inch (12") fulcrum rather than the fourteen-inch (14") fulcrum used on the Lorythmic Scale. Also, instead of using the alpha-numeric designation of the Lorythmic Scale, the Official Scale directly indicates the amount of weight, in ounces, required at the butt end of the grip to balance the moment of the club about the twelve-inch (12") balance point. The Official Scale was never adopted by the golf club industry as a method of matching clubs.

The term swingweight is a misnomer. What is referred to as

swingweight actually represents a static condition. It is the first moment, in engineering terms, that is the product of the weight of the entire golf club times the distance of the center of gravity of the club is from a point fourteen inches (14") from the extreme butt end of the grip. This moment is normally expressed in inch-ounces (distance in inches times weight in ounces). For ease in reading the scale, an alpha numeric designation was applied to reflect the moment values and thus the terms D-0, C-8, etc., were born. Since the swingweight fulcrum is fourteen (14") from the butt end of the grip, it doesn't really reflect the dead weight feel to the golfer whose hands are near the top end of the grip. On the basis of a theoretical two-lever system for a golf swing, the static feel of the club should be approximately four inches (4") from the butt end, where the two hands meet.

Until some time after graphite shafts were introduced, most driver heads were made of wood and weighed about seven and one-quarter ounces. The heads were fitted with steel shafts that weighed about four and one-quarter ounces and grips that weigh slightly less than two ounces. These are approximate values since the weight of a steel shaft, for example, will vary depending on its diameter and stiffness. Still, the difference in weight between a stiff shaft and a regular shaft is no more than three to four grams (1/8 ounce). Taking the sum of the components, most drivers had a total weight of 13.25 to 13.50 ounces. Since the weight of the shaft and grip was always close to 6–1/8 ounces, any difference in swing weight really reflected the difference in head weight. Therefore, the old swingweight scales served fairly well to show the weight distribution difference between golf clubs equipped with steel shafts. A specified swingweight was then used to match all the clubs in the set. There were a few who advocated matching irons two swingweight points less than the woods in a complete set of clubs. However, those that did were in the minority. The alpha-numeric designations of the Lorythmic swingweight scale that are used for most of the men's clubs have been in the D-0 to D-2 range.

The reason for the use of the fourteen-inch (14") fulcrum

remains a mystery to this day. There is no known rationale to justify this feature. For example, because the grip is located on the opposite side of the fulcrum from the head of the golf club, even the weight of the tape used to build up the grip size will lower the swingweight. This means that even though the overall weight of the club is increased the swing-weight will be reduced.

As mentioned earlier, at times lead tape is applied under the grip to reduce the swing weight when matching a set of clubs. In other cases lead shot has been tamped down in the hosel of irons to increase the swingweight for club matching purposes. In neither case will the flight of the golf ball be affected much since there has not been any change in the clubhead that makes contact with the ball. If a golf club that is to have a swingweight equal to D-2 is placed on the balance prior to the installation of the grip, the scale reading will be E-0 to E-2, ten points higher than the reading as a complete golf club. Despite the 8 to 10 point difference the actual feel of the clubhead will not change much because the grip is under the hands. It is readily apparent, then, that just because each club in the set has the same swingweight that all the clubs will not feel the same. Note that we have been discussing feel under static conditions.

Shafts made of composite materials such as graphite and boron are now very popular. These shafts are appreciably lighter than shafts fabricated of steel. The first graphite shafts weighed about three ounces. At the time of this writing, there are composite shafts that weigh as little as two ounces and yet have the stiffness of steel shafts. These lighter shafts change the overall weight of the club by a significant amount. However, since the center of gravity of the shaft is only seven to eight inches from the fourteen-inch (14") fulcrum of the of the swingweight scale, the change to a lighter shaft does not alter the swingweight scale reading very much: perhaps three to four points. A steel-shafted D-0 driver will usually become C-7 if refitted with a graphite shaft. It is a common practice in industry to make the head of a driver which is equipped with a graphite shaft about seven grams heavier than the head of a similar club with a steel shaft in order to bring it back to a D-0 or D-1 swingweight. A good question is, what is magic about D-0 or your "favorite" swingweight number?

As discussed earlier, before steel shafts were introduced in the late 1920s, golf club shafts were made of hickory wood. A raw 44-inch hickory shaft weighs more than eight ounces (230 grams). By the time the wood shaft is sanded and varnished, it still weighs more than seven ounces. To keep the overall weight of the club at what was considered a reasonable value, the head had to be quite light; therefore the finished club did not have much feel. When I played in the Hickory Hacker's Tournaments I found that because of the lighter heads I lost about twenty yards with each club. If the wood shaft was made lighter, it would not only become too flexible but it would also have unacceptable torque characteristics. This is one reason why the golf swing of the wood shaft era was far different from the modern swing. To put it another way, the modern swing was made possible by the lighter and much more rigid steel shaft.

There is little doubt that the arbitrary swingweight criteria as a design standard for the manufacture and matching of golf clubs is obsolete for this high tech era. The new lightweight and ultra lightweight composite shafts call for a reassessment of how different components relate to each other. The real benefits of lightweight shafts will not be realized as long as clubheads continue to be designed to steel shaft standards. Rather than adding weights to the heads that are to be equipped with graphite shafts, the weight of the head might better be reduced. When this is done it will result in greater clubhead speed for the same physical effort. The added clubhead speed will more than compensate for the reduced head weight. This, in turn, should result in greater distance. Head feel will not be lost when lighter composite shafts are used, if the shaft is not too stiff.

As for matching clubs in a set, a true swingweight method should be introduced. Swinging a golf club is a dynamic situation. Therefore, the new system should be based on a dynamic criterion rather than the static measurement of the first moment that has been used. A more logical system would be based on the moment of inertia, the second moment, of the entire club about a point about four inches (4") from the butt end of the club.

Several devices for measuring the moment of inertia directly were patented some years ago. To my knowledge none of these were ever accepted by anyone in the industry. A set of irons matched in this manner would have the clubheads of the long irons lighter than they are at present and the heads of the short irons heavier than they are now. On the Lorythmic Scale, each iron would vary approximately one swingweight point from its neighbor. Sets of clubs, each set with different constant value for the moment of inertia, would be fabricated to accommodate the strength and/or ability of a particular golfer much as different swingweight values have been used in the past.

While I was employed as a consultant with one company in Carlsbad, California, we fabricated three sets of clubs according to specifications I provided. The value of the moment of inertia was constant for each iron in the set but the constant value was different for each set. When each set of clubs was tested on a frequency measuring device, we found that the frequency was exactly the same for every iron in that set from the two iron through the wedge. This happened because by removing some weight from the longer irons we increased the stiffness of the shaft, and when weight was added to the shorter irons we reduced the stiffness of those shafts. Keeping the MOI constant for each set provided the data for the weight of each clubhead. In ordinary sets built with a constant swingweight, the frequency varies for each club in the set. This means that the shaft stiffness is different for each club.

The term "frequency matched irons" has been used for some time for golf clubs where there is a uniform *difference* in frequency between the clubs in the set. This was accomplished by careful selection of the shafts. To put it another way, the allowable tolerance for the shafts in the frequency matched sets is much smaller than for run of the mill shafts but they do not have the same frequency.

I do not believe that a player would, at first, be aware of the difference between a set of clubs matched by swingweight and a set matched by using a constant MOI. However in time the player using the constant MOI golf clubs will become more consistent and hit fewer poor shots. He or she will also do a better job of taking the game from the practice range to the golf course.

In deriving the equation for the MOI of a golf club about a point four inches (4") from the butt end of the club, I found that the effect of the grip was negligible and could be ignored. This is the case since the center of gravity of the grip is very close to the four inch axis that is used. By contrast, as mentioned earlier, the grip can affect the swingweight by as much as ten (10) swingweight points. It is not difficult to calculate the swingweight of each club within a set that has a constant MOI. This might be convenient for manufacturing purposes.

MATCHING GOLF CLUBS:
THE WAY IT SHOULD BE DONE

What is a matched set of golf clubs? Is it limited to one in which all of the clubs look pretty much alike and have the same swing-weight? If that were the case shaft flexibility would not be a factor. Therefore the clubs in a so-called "matched set" are equipped with shafts the have the same degree of flexibility for a given length. Most sets of clubs for men are fitted with shafts that have the same designation (such as *A, R, S or X*). These letters denote the relative stiffness of the shaft in ascending order. Some of the shaft manu-facturers use numbers to represent the relative stiffness rather than letters. There have also been some shafts sold with stiffness ratings using the terms: *firm, strong,* etc.

The public has been led to believe that clubs are matched if all the clubs in the set look alike, have the same swingweight and are equipped with shafts that are similarly marked. The golfer thinks that the clubs in the set will feel same and swing the same. This is not the case. If it were, then any golfer would be able to hit long irons as easily as he or she hits the short irons. The clubs are not matched with regard to feel. At best, while the clubs do not feel the same, they vary uniformly from one club to the next. Again, it is no wonder that many golfers find it difficult to take their game from the practice range to the golf course.

With this introduction, let us look into what is involved in a matching process. For example, what are the allowable tolerances for head weight, shaft stiffness and shaft weight for a set of golf clubs? Are the tolerances small enough that the difference from club to club vary uniformly? You will see that this depends not only on the club maker's quality control, but also on the type of shaft used.

When we look at a golf club we see that it is composed of three parts: the head, the shaft, and the grip. But how do the clubs in the set vary from one another? By now you know that the industry standard for length is one-half inch difference between club numbers for both woods and irons. The one exception may be the driver. A player may choose to have his driver more than an inch longer than the three wood. It may not be a wise choice but it is sometimes done.

As the shaft length increases, the player must stand farther from the ball. Therefore the lie angle should also vary accordingly. It was pointed out elsewhere how the lie of the club can affect the direction of the golf shot. It is important enough to repeat for emphasis that every golfer should have the lie of his or her clubs checked to make certain that the lie of each club fits that particular golfer's address position. In my opinion, the largest errors may be found among women golfers, who are using clubs that are too long for them.

As mentioned earlier, the golf industry uses "swingweight" as the criterion for matching clubs. To repeat, this means that the product of the total weight of the club and the distance from the center of gravity of the club from a point located fourteen inches from the butt end of the grip is the same for each club in the set. This is the definition of swingweight. Since each club in the set has a different length, it follows that as the club length decreases, the head weight must increase. For woods, each one-half inch that the shaft is shortened approximately five grams must be added to the weight of the head. For irons, the difference in weight is usually about seven grams. The value depends on the distance of the center of gravity of the club from the fourteen-inch balance point. In a typical set of irons, the head of a two iron weighs about 246 grams. Head weight then increase seven grams per club so that the head weight of the pitching wedge will weigh close to 302 grams.

Naturally, the heads in a set will resemble each other in appearance, as if they belong to the same family. This might be called "user friendly." It cannot be helped that, at address, the straight blade of a two iron looks different than the more lofted short irons. It will help most golfers if there is a strong resemblance between all the clubs in a set.

There isn't much that can or should be said about the grips. Naturally they will all look alike. However, grips are not manufactured to close tolerances and there can be several grams difference between grips of the same kind. Any difference will make the swing weight vary. The grip is on the opposite side of the fourteen-inch balance point from the center of gravity of the club. Therefore, even though the addition of the grip increases the total weight of the club, it lowers the swing weight a great deal. Unless the grips are sorted so that uniform weight grips are used in a set, the swing weight may vary. For example, a full cord grip may weigh as much as eight grams less than a solid composition grip. Even the tape used under the grip affects the swingweight. When a grip is built up to an oversize value for golfers with big hands, the added tape required for the build up reduces the swingweight. The only real problem here is what the manufacturers or repair technicians do if they try to bring the club back to the original swingweight. The golfer will not realize any difference in swingweight that occurs in connection with the grip because all of these changes occur under the hands and does not affect the moment of inertia or feel of the club.

It is my opinion that the shaft is the most important part of the golf club. A player holds the golf club in his or her hands, thus the feel of the clubhead is transmitted to the player through the shaft. For this reason, shaft uniformity in a set is of paramount importance. Unfortunately, this is the place where problems are most likely to occur. We have already mentioned that shafts are sorted using designations such as X, S, R, etc. For steel shafts that use these letter classifications, the manufacturer's weight tolerances are plus or minus 3/16 of an ounce. This means that in any group of "R" shafts, for example, there can be as much as 3/8 of an ounce difference in weight between any two shafts: almost 11 grams, nearly ten percent.

Since shafts that weigh more are stiffer, it is important that shafts be sorted by weight before they are fitted with clubheads. The frequency matched shafts we referred to earlier are manufactured to a tolerance of plus or minus 1/32 of an ounce. This is 1/6 of the tolerance permitted in the type of shafts designated by letters. When a golf club is gripped in a clamp or vise and made to vibrate, the frequency of vibration varies directly with the stiffness of the shaft (all other things being equal). Since each club in the set has a different length, each club will have a different frequency if the set is matched by swingweight. In a set of golf clubs matched by swingweight the clubs with shorter shafts vibrate faster than those with longer shafts. To repeat, "frequency" matching does not mean that all the clubs vibrate with the same frequency. It implies that the frequency difference between clubs is uniform. Table 5 contains the data on a set of irons I used that were equipped with frequency matched (FM 6.0) shafts. The frequency differential between any two adjoining irons is 6 to 7 cycles per minute (cpm).

TABLE 5
FREQUENCIES FOR A SET OF IRONS WITH CONSTANT SWING WEIGHT

IRON	Head Weight (grams)	Total Weight (grams)	Frequency	Frequency (cycles/sec)
2	246	397	326	5.43
3	253	402	331	5.51
4	260	408	337	5.62
5	267	412	343	5.72
6	274	417	348	5.80
7	281	423	353	5.88
8	288	431	360	6.10
9	295	434	366	6.10
PW	302	442	372	6.20

Shaft stiffness is a relative term, a comparative tool. When we increase the weight of the clubhead, the shaft will deflect more and therefore acts as if it were less stiff. By the same token, if we start with similar shafts and shorten them (as in a set of irons with parallel tip shafts) the shorter shafts will be stiffer as the length decreases.

Steel shafts are manufactured two ways: with tapered tips or with parallel tips. Tapered tip shafts are manufactured in different lengths in 1/2 inch increments. If trimming is required, it is done from the butt end of the shaft. Conversely, parallel tip shafts are generally provided in one length. The parallel tip shafts are trimmed at the tip end. Most sets of clubs are equipped with parallel tip shafts and, therefore, have progressively shorter parallel tip (smallest diameter) sections as the irons become shorter. This makes the shorter irons much stiffer than the longer irons.

There are other possibilities for matching clubs that would improve the end product. For one thing it makes more sense to use a balance point that is closer to where the club is gripped by the player. Four to five inches from the butt end of the club would seem to be the logical choice rather than fourteen inches as used on the Lorythmic and Prorythmic balances.

A dynamic criterion comes much closer to representing what the player feels as he or she swings the golf club. Matching clubs to a constant MOI would improve the feel that the golfer senses. To repeat, if this method were employed, the heads of the longer clubs would be lighter while the heads of shorter clubs would be heavier. While the change would not be drastic, it would make the clubs feel more like each other during the swing.

As an example, let us say that you have a set of irons where each club has a swingweight equal to D-2. Suppose that your favorite iron is the six iron and you would like to have all the irons in the set feel like this six iron. That means that the other clubs in the set must have the same MOI as the six iron. If this were done the two iron would have a swingweight value of C-8.4 and the nine iron a swingweight value of D-5.3. If we round off these numbers to whole point values, we would have a C-8 two iron and let the swingweight of each successive iron increase by one point until we reach a swingweight of D-5 for the nine iron. This would make the long irons easier to use. I am convinced that if a golfer used a set of clubs that were matched in the manner that was described here, in time he or she would become more consistent. Equally as important it will result in the golfer doing a better job of taking his game from the practice range to the golf course.

There are some golfers that prefer heavier clubs because it helps them to slow down their backswing. Sam Snead used D-5 or D-6 clubs. George Bayer swung a wood in the "E" range. This is pointed out merely to say that there is no magic in the D-0 to D-2 range. The elements of the golf swing should be the same, but not necessarily the equipment. The physical condition of a player makes a difference when choosing the weight of golf club that he or she should swing. I am quite sure that the better women golfers do not swing a C-5 club. At one of the clubs I played at in the San Diego area we had a low handicap woman golfer who used men's clubs very effectively. However, she was tall and athletic and the clubs fit her. On several occasions her drives were longer than mine from the same tees. I tried to tell myself that it was because she was thirty years younger than I was. Of course I lost that argument. Beware of the golf clubs in the inventory of a store that are just "right" for you. Remember, you are unique and this would be quite a coincidence.

I would like to see the problem of quality control improved by all golf club manufacturers. It is unfortunate that such a large a part of the price of a golf club is spent on advertising and endorsements. I would like to see more of it put into providing a better product.

THE SHAFT AND ITS ROLE

The only thing that determines the outcome of the golf shot is the clubhead. Distance is a direct function of the clubhead velocity at impact. The trajectory or shape of the golf shot is dependent upon the loft of the clubhead, the alignment of the face at impact and the path of the clubhead at the moment of impact. If the clubhead were to be disconnected from the shaft a fraction of a millisecond before impact, the flight of the golf ball would not be affected. This was proven as part of a research project sponsored by the Golf Society of Great Britain during the 1960s. High speed photographs of the impact, using a driver, with the head and shaft connected only by a hinge pin, clearly showed that the position of the head with respect to the shaft did not change during impact. (The Search for the Perfect Swing, J.B. Lippincott Co., pp. 146–147.)

Based on this fact, what is the role of the shaft? The role of the shaft is to deliver the clubhead to the ball in a manner that will produce the result that the player intended. The shaft is the communication link between the player and the clubhead. Some people believe that the shaft transmits power to the golf ball. This is not the case. To demonstrate this, consider that shaft stiffness can be measured on a deflection board with the butt end of the shaft rigidly fixed and a small weight attached to the tip end of the shaft that is left free to deflect. The weight will deflect the tip of the shaft three or more inches depending on the stiffness of the shaft. This is more than the shaft is deflected by a tour player during any part of the swing with a driver. It is obvious that if the golfer doesn't cause the shaft to deflect as much as a small weight, then it cannot be delivering the kind of power required to drive a golf ball 300 yards and create a ball/clubhead impact force in excess of 2000 pounds.

As stated before, the main function of the shaft is to deliver the clubhead to the ball. However, as the communication link between the player and the clubhead, the shaft should tell the golfer what is happening to the clubhead during the swing. If the player has the correct shaft for his kind of swing, it will help his timing. While the feel that a golfer does experience is primarily due to the weight of the clubhead, the weight of the shaft is also a contributing factor. There is less feel with a steel shaft than with a lightweight graphite shaft. This is analogous to a fishing rod. For bait casting with a heavy lure, a short and fairly stiff fishing rod is appropriate. A fly rod, though, is considerably lighter, longer, and has a finely tapered tip since not much more than the weight of the line is to be sensed.

Another component of feel may be that of a minor imbalance. This imbalance is due to the fact that the clubhead's center of gravity is offset from the axis of both the shaft and the grip. The torsional moment of inertia of the golf club is quite small since the center of gravity of the clubhead is about two inches from the longitudinal axis of the shaft. Therefore this imbalance is not a significant factor.

On the basis of what has been said to this point, one might wonder why we must have shafts of varying stiffness, different flex points, and different torsional characteristics. With regard to stiffness, the important reason is to offset the effect of centrifugal force. Centrifugal force is created whenever any mass moves along a curved path. Every automobile driver feels centrifugal force when making a sharp turn. Race tracks are banked to compensate for centrifugal force. Centrifugal force keeps spacecraft in orbit. The magnitude of the centrifugal force that is created is proportional to the amount of mass and the square of its velocity. It is also inversely proportional to the radius of curvature at any instant. In the case of a clubhead during the downswing, its path is nearly circular, particularly just before and just after impact. Therefore centrifugal force is present.

We will quantify the amount of centrifugal force that is developed when a driver is being used by players of different abilities. Table 6 is the result of calculations of centrifugal force covering a range of clubhead speeds from 70 to 130 miles per hour. Two different radii were used in the calculations. One radius represents the length of the driver, 43 inches. This is approximately the radius of curvature in the impact area when a driver is being swung by a good golfer who has a late release. The second radius is the sum of the club length and the player's arm length. This is the swing radius for a player who uncocks his or her wrists early during the downswing, sometimes referred to as casting. Arm length here is defined as the distance from the left wrist to the player's center of rotation, a point halfway between the shoulders, approximately 34 inches. Therefore the second radius that is used here is 77 inches. The driver in this example has a 200 gram (7.05 ounce) head. To simplify matters, the additional component of centrifugal force due to the shaft is small and, therefore, ignored in the calculations.

TABLE 6
CENTRIFUGAL FORCE VS. CLUBHEAD SPEED

Clubhead Velocity (mph)	Centrifugal Force (pounds) R = 43 inches	Centrifugal Force (pounds) R = 67 inches
70	40.4	25.9
80	52.7	33.8
90	66.7	42.8
100	82.3	52.8
110	99.7	64.0
120	118.5	76.1
130	139.2	89.3

Table 6 shows that the centrifugal force for players with a late release can be approximately 80 percent greater than for those that uncock their wrists early during the downswing. The magnitude of the centrifugal force is substantial even at clubhead speeds of 90 miles per hour. For both woods and irons, the center of gravity of the clubhead is not located in line with the axis of the shaft. Center-shafted woods and irons are not permitted under the rules. Consequently, the strong pull of the centrifugal force created by the clubhead and acting through its center of gravity creates a moment that will cause the shaft to bend. In the case of an iron with its thin head, the centrifugal force due to clubhead tends to bend the shaft in only one direction: toe-down. The amount of toe- down deflection is proportional to the magnitude of the centrifugal force and the stiffness of the shaft. This bending has the effect of opening the club face in much the same manner as that which occurs when a player is faced with a sidehill lie where the ball is below the player's feet. A stiff shaft minimizes the amount of toe-down bending that takes place and is therefore one of the factors for making a stiff shaft the choice of a strong player.

The center of gravity for a wood clubhead is located both behind the axis and toward the toe. Therefore the bending of the shaft due to centrifugal force occurs in two directions. Not only does the shaft bend in the toe-down direction, as in the case of the iron, but it also bends in the forward direction perpendicular to the face of the clubhead. This tends to both increase the loft and to make the club "look" to the right. Again, a stiff shaft will minimize these effects and is the second factor for making a stiff shaft the choice of the strong player. This also explains why a softer shaft helps the weaker player to get the ball into the air more easily with a wood. During the swing the effective loft becomes greater than the design loft built into the clubhead.

Photographs that show the shaft bent forward just before impact have led to the erroneous belief that this represents the release of the shaft bending that occurred at the beginning of the downswing. It is not difficult to understand that this is not the case as soon as one realizes that the shaft bending that occurs at the top of the backswing/beginning of the downswing is parallel to the club face. The bending that is observed prior to impact for a wood is perpendicular to the club face. Therefore it cannot be the result of recovery from the earlier deflection. Stroboscope pictures of a complete golf swing show that the shaft becomes straight shortly after the beginning of the downswing.

In bending, a metal shaft that is stiffer will also have greater torsional rigidity. Shafts made of composite materials (such as carbon fiber impregnated with a resinous material) vary in strength, both in bending and in torsion, depending on how the fibers are laid up. Naturally, every shaft is expected to be fully elastic under all conditions that may be experienced during use, including clubhead contact with the ground.

Much is made of the importance of torsional rigidity (usually referred to as torque) in shafts. As I mentioned earlier, torque is the couple or moment applied to a body. The term "torque resistance" is more accurate. Torque and torsional rigidity are engineering or physics terms to represent a twisting force and the ability to resist torque, respectively.

Many readers may have heard about the importance of this torque resistance in shafts. Some believe that the torsional rigidity of the shaft is important when off-center contact with the ball occurs. In the first paragraph of this chapter I mentioned that the golf shot would not be affected if the head were disconnected from the shaft just prior to impact. This is true in the case of off-center contact as well as central impact. There is no doubt that a more rigid shaft will resist torque better than a weaker shaft when the grip end of the shaft is held in a vise. However, this is not the situation encountered under actual playing conditions. During play a good player does not grip the club tightly, as we discussed earlier. In fact, the player does the opposite in order to be able to release the club freely as it approaches impact. Further, the player is holding the club in hands that are composed of fleshy material in contrast to the unforgiving metal grip of a testing machine or vise. Since the duration of impact with the ball lasts no longer than one-half millisecond (0.0005 seconds), the ball is off the face of the club before the player senses the feedback that signals an off-center impact. The player is not able to compensate for what has occurred. As long as the shaft has sufficient rigidity to resist the effect of the slight eccentricity of the center of gravity of the clubhead, additional torsional rigidity is not important.

Whenever a player uses a stiff "S" steel shaft he automatically has a shaft that has more torsional rigidity than a regular "R" shaft. However, this is not the case for graphite shafts. The reason for this is that graphite shafts are made up of fibers. The strength of the composite material lies in the direction of the fibers. Perpendicular to the fibers, the material is only as strong as the resin that bonds the fibers. Therefore, the torsional rigidity of a graphite shaft is dependent on how the fibers are lined up in the lay up.

A player cannot apply torque to the shaft during the golf swing. In order for torque to be present, there must be resistance. There is nothing present to resist rotation of the clubhead prior to impact.

From the days of the wood shafts to the present, the shaft remains the most important part of the golf club. A good golf swing is a matter of feel and a properly fitted shaft is the feel communicator. If a player who does not develop much clubhead speed were to use a shaft with little or no flexibility, he would not sense much, if any, feel of the clubhead. This player would have a strictly mechanical golf swing and would, suffer from irregular timing as a result. Also, he or she might experience difficulty getting the ball into the air. There is, then, a relationship between clubhead speed developed by the player and the optimum shaft stiffness for a player's clubs. The average lady golfer—not tournament players—will probably have a clubhead speed below 70 miles per hour and she will need the softest shaft available to sense the feel of the clubhead. The same may be true for a senior golfer who is well past his prime. His clubhead speed will probably be in the 70–80 miles per hour range. This senior player might be better off with an "A" shaft. For players who develop clubhead speeds between 80–95 miles per hour an "R" shaft will probably suit them best. Those with a driver clubhead speed of 95–105 miles per hour should choose an "S" shaft. The enviable golfers that attain a clubhead speed in excess of 105 miles per hour will no doubt be happiest with an "X" shaft. To a weak golfer an "X" shaft would have the feel of a utility pole.

The matter of quality in shafts is important, whether you are dealing with steel shafts or graphite shafts. High quality shafts are a worthwhile investment.

CLUBHEAD WEIGHT:
EFFECT ON DISTANCE

The majority of male golfers play with clubs that are in the D-0 to D-2 swingweight range. This will generally apply to both the woods and the irons. Since the driver is the club that is used for maximum distance, the effect of adding or subtracting weight from the driver clubhead will be examined.

We know that swingweight is the static moment of a golf club about a point fourteen (14) inches from the butt end of the grip. As mentioned before, the static balance referred to here is the first moment of the total weight of the golf club about a fourteen-inch balance point. The value of the moment is expressed in inch ounces. The alpha numeric designation, D-0 swingweight, actually represents a moment of 213.5 inch ounces. Each point on the swingweight balance represents a static moment change of 1.75 inch ounces. A golf club with a swing weight of D-2 has a moment equal to 217.0 inch ounces while for a C-0 golf club, the moment is 196.0 inch ounces.

A golf club is made up of three components the head, the shaft, and the grip. Each of these components makes a contribution to the swing weight in proportion to its weight and the distance of its center of gravity from the fourteen-inch balance point. Since the clubhead makes up more than half the total weight of the club and its center of gravity is farthest from the balance point, it has the greatest effect on the swingweight of the club. The grip is on the opposite side of the balance point from the center of gravity of the shaft and clubhead. Therefore the grip makes a negative contribution to the swingweight of the golf club.

In order to achieve a D-0 to D-2 swingweight, the weight of the head must be in the neighborhood of 200 grams, which is a little more than seven ounces. The weight of the clubhead will vary depending on the type of shaft involved and also on its length. Steel shafts are much heavier than graphite shafts and for that reason the head of a driver that is fitted to a steel shaft is lighter than one that is fitted to a graphite shaft if the same swingweight is to be achieved. There are even substantial differences in the weights of shafts made from the same material, depending on the stiffness of the shaft. The weight of the head is then adjusted accordingly. The manner in which it is done today has not changed over the years.

The initial velocity of a golf ball following impact depends entirely on the weight of the clubhead and its velocity at impact. Nothing else affects the initial velocity of the ball with the exception of its coefficient of restitution. Tests have shown that the distance that the ball will carry in still air is directly proportional to the initial ball velocity and, therefore, to the clubhead speed. Long hitters can generate clubhead speeds in excess of 115 miles per hour, or 168 feet per second. This is due to the efficiency of their golf swings and the speed that they move their bodies.

First we will examine what would happen if the weight of the clubhead could be increased without changing the clubhead velocity. The mathematical equation for initial golf ball velocity is:

$V = U (1+e)/(1+ m/M)$ where

V = initial velocity of the golf ball

M = weight of the clubhead

m = weight of the golf ball

U = clubhead speed just prior to impact

e = coefficient of restitution between the golf ball and the clubhead

From robot tests using a 90 compression ball on an ordinary

driver, "e" was calculated to be 0.77 at a clubhead speed of 100 miles per hour. The value of "e" will be smaller at higher clubhead speeds and larger as the clubhead speed decreases. For example the value of "e" is about 0.81 when using a putter. The reason for this is that since the head speed of the putter is small the golf ball will not be flattened as much during impact and there is less energy loss.

Table 7 shows the result of calculations for "V," the launch velocity of the golf ball, at a constant clubhead speed of 100 miles per hour for clubhead weights varying from 6 ounces to 1000 ounces.

TABLE 7 EFFECT OF CLUBHEAD WEIGHT ON GOLF BALL LAUNCH VELOCITY AT CONSTANT CLUBHEAD SPEED OF 100 MPH		
Clubhead Weight, M (ounces)	Launch Velocity, v (feet per second)	Percent increase Over 7 oz. Clubhead
6.0	204	-2.4
7.0	209	0
8.0	214	2.4
9.0	219	4.8
10.0	222	6.2
12.0	227	8.6
16.0	230	12.0
50.0	234	20.0
100.0	251	21.5
1000.0	258	23.4

It can be seen from Table 7 that the initial golf ball velocity increases by 2.4 percent when the clubhead weight is increased by one ounce from 6 to 7 or 7 to 8 ounces. The amount of increase in initial golf ball velocity becomes less as each additional ounce is added. While the effect of adding one ounce (from 7 to 8 ounces) changes the initial golf ball velocity by 2.4 percent, increasing the weight by 50 ounces (from 50 to 100 ounces) adds only 1.5 percent. A further increase of 900 ounces contributes a mere 1.9 percent.

On the other hand, increasing the clubhead weight will have an adverse effect on the clubhead speed that can be generated by the golfer. This is due to the increase in the dynamic moment of inertia of the golf club as a whole when weight is added to the clubhead. As mentioned earlier readers know this from swinging a heavy warm-up club. The loss of clubhead speed will more than offset the benefit of added weight and a loss of distance will occur. The decrease in clubhead speed due to added weight is a complex matter because we are now dealing with the matter of available energy that a particular player can supply to the golf swing. It also depends on the efficiency of the individual player's swing. Naturally, the expert player swings a golf club far more efficiently than the average golfer. Because the expert golfer's swing is finely tuned, he will be affected somewhat more by changes in the clubhead weight than the high handicap golfer. However, the clubhead speed of the expert golfer is much greater to start with. Table 8 lists typical values of clubhead speed for various classes of golfers when swinging a driver with a seven ounce clubhead.

TABLE 8
TYPICAL CLUBHEAD SPEED FOR VARIOUS CLASSES OF GOLFERS

Class of Golfer	Clubhead Speed Miles per Hour
Touring Pro	115
Low Handicap	105
High Handicap	90
Beginner	85

While the decrease in clubhead speed is not directly proportional to the increase in clubhead weight, the assumption of a linear relationship in the six to eight ounce range of clubhead weights will yield fairly close results. This being the case, it is possible to write algebraic equations for the change in clubhead speeds for the four classes of golfers listed in Table 8 as a function of added clubhead weight. Table 9 lists the approximate change in clubhead speed that might be expected for each ounce of clubhead weight that is added or subtracted for the four classes of golfers.

TABLE 9
CHANGE IN CLUBHEAD SPEED FOR EACH OUNCE OF CHANGE IN CLUBHEAD WEIGHT

Class of Golfer	Change in MPH
Touring Pro	3.5
Low Handicap	2.5
High Handicap	2.0
Beginner	1.5

The above values are typical for different classes of golfers. We already know that there are a number of touring professionals and others who can swing a seven ounce clubhead faster than 115 miles per hour. For clubhead weights less than seven ounces, an increase in speed will result. It is more than likely that a golfer could hit a drive farther with a lighter clubhead because the added energy transmitted to the ball as a result of the greater clubhead speed would more than offset the loss due to lower clubhead weight.

The general equation for kinetic energy is:

Kinetic energy = $\frac{1}{2} M v^2$

In this equation the energy is proportional to the first power of the mass but the second power of the velocity. Therefore it is possible that more distance will be obtained from employing a lighter clubhead, because for the same muscular effort a golfer can achieve greater clubhead speed. In summary, additional clubhead speed will result in a greater benefit than increased clubhead weight.

As mentioned earlier, it has been determined from actual field tests, using a robot, that for a particular driver, carry of the golf ball is proportional to the initial golf ball velocity. Design variables such as loft and center of gravity location will affect the amount of backspin created and these, in turn, will also affect carry and overall distance.

There are some newer drivers on the market that have ports built into the head so that it is possible to change the weight of the head by inserting weights made of metals with different densities. The golfer can experiment with these clubs to find the best head weight for that individual. It is possible that the golfer may find that he or she does not like the feel of a lighter clubhead. Habit is a difficult thing to break. Another factor that enters into the matter of changing the weight of the head is that the player will sense a different feel in the stiffness of the shaft, as explained earlier.

A LITTLE OF THIS AND THAT

The rules of golf allow you to carry a maximum of fourteen clubs in your bag. The penalty is severe for a violation of this rule. If you break a club during ordinary normal play, you may replace that club. If the club is broken in a fit of anger or carelessness, the club may not be replaced. You may change the golf clubs in your bag between rounds but not during a single round.

When you plan a shot, decide on the kind of shot you feel confident that you can execute. Especially in stroke play tournaments do not try to make the shot that you wish you could make.

If you have practiced the type of golf shot that is required, let your subconscious guide the actual execution of the shot. Don't get in your own way with mechanics.

I once heard Bob Toski remark about the tension that can set in from "paralysis from over analysis." There is a lot to that.

If you get into trouble your next shot should be the one that will get you out of trouble. This is the way to avoid double and triple bogeys. It is not a good idea to "go for broke."

Always approach the ball you are going to hit from behind the ball. By doing this the last thing recorded on your brain is a picture of the planned route to your target.

Keep your clubs clean, including the grooves.

Wear sun block and reapply it a few times during a round of golf.

Keep your golf ball clean or it will not roll true on the greens.

A golf ball may not have its center of gravity at its geometric center. It can be tested by using any heavy liquid solution that will float the ball. A small jar with glycerin added to the water is one way to do this. Place a mark on the ball so that you will be able to see if the ball remains in whatever position you place it the mixture. If the ball tends to rotate the center of gravity is off center and the ball will not roll true on the green.

On a very cold day it is a good idea to carry one or two extra balls in your pocket to keep them warm. Then change balls on every hole. A cold ball will not travel as far as a warm ball.

Keep your grips tacky. Wipe them with a damp cloth regularly.

On the putting surface be very careful to avoid stepping on the putting line of any other player.

Do not stand directly in front of or behind a person that is putting or directly behind someone hitting any golf shot.

If you have a caddie, you are responsible for the behavior of your caddie during the play of a round.

Golf courses are the only things that I can think of where man has improved on nature. This is particularly true if you look at most western American golf courses, particularly those in the desert southwest, such as Palm Springs, Las Vegas, and even San Diego, where brown hills have been converted to verdant golf courses. The great golf courses of Great Britain are the links courses, which have been fashioned from tidal land. When it comes to Pebble Beach, I am willing to call it a draw.

Any person who goes out to play golf should know and understand the rules of golf and golf etiquette. A golfer will both respect and enjoy the game of golf more when he or she is aware of the rules and etiquette pertaining to the game. If you are really into golf, I suggest that you obtain a copy of the "Rules and Decisions" from the United States Golf Association. You will find that the number of possibilities for interpretation of the Rules of Golf is nearly infinite. In addition to being informative, I found that reading the Rules and Decisions was entertaining, and on occasion hilarious. I recall one case where it was reported that the ball rolled into a drain pipe where the entry to the drain was out of bounds. However, where the ball came to rest in the drain, the ball was in bounds. This was a decision for Solomon.

The game of golf is said to be a game for ladies and gentlemen. Unlike other sports there are no referees or umpires present to supervise the play. Following the rules of golf is somewhat like being on the honor system. When playing golf, players are expected to call penalties on themselves whether it is observed by anyone else or not.

Golf is often played with a side bet going on. If the bet is small, where the amount of stakes is not important, it can add a little zest to game. It may even help to make a player concentrate more. However, if the stakes are such that the money involved becomes important, golf is no longer a game; it is gambling. Personally, I have no respect for people who use golf as a vehicle for gambling.

The Rules of Golf are now the same worldwide. The United States Golf Association is the governing body for the rules of golf in the United States and its territories and for Mexico. The Royal and Ancient Golf Club of St. Andrews has the same authority for the rest of the world. Until quite recently, the two ruling bodies were not in total agreement. Past differences showed up when Americans played in British tournaments as well as during international matches. Earlier, this included differences in the size of the golf ball and the use of center-shafted putters. However, at present, the rules of both bodies are in agreement.

The Rules of Golf as issued by the U.S.G.A. include the subject of golf etiquette. Observance of golf etiquette means that the player is being considerate for the rights of others on the golf course as well as the players in his or her own group.

In order to keep the flow of the play at a reasonable rate, a player should prepare for his next shot while awaiting his turn provided that it does not disturb any other player on the golf course. One of the expressions I picked up, years ago, from golf course marshals in Scotland was, "you must keep your place on the golf course." This translates into "be sure you stay one golf shot behind the people ahead of you." While you must be careful not to hit into the group ahead of you, do hit your shot as soon as they are out of range.

There is also the matter of safety. The clubhead of a golf club traveling at near 100 miles per hour or a golf ball traveling at even higher speed can be a lethal weapon. Every person in the group should make certain that he or she stands behind the line of the ball of any player preparing to hit a golf shot. A toed golf shot can travel at nearly 90 degrees to the player's intended line of flight.

Whenever I went out to play golf I always tried to leave the golf course in better condition than I found it. This means that I raked the bunker carefully before I left. If some other player left the bunker in less than the best condition, I took the time to repair that place as well.

When I arrive at the putting green, I make it my business to look for ball marks that someone else may have missed. Before leaving the green, it is a good idea to look for spike marks or other minor damage to the putting surface and tamp them down. No one should ever try to remove the ball from the cup with the head of a putter. This can damage the edge of the hole. Also, great care should be taken when tending or removing the pin from the cup.

The provisional ball rule is a great timesaver when you think a ball may be out-of-bounds or lost. It is a long trip back to the tee after a fruitless search for your ball or after finding it out of bounds. It also slows up the game for the players in your group or those following you. You must announce that you are playing a provisional ball when choosing that option. If you do locate your errant shot on the golf course but find that it is unplayable, you may not play the provisional ball. You must continue with the original ball. This was not always so but it is now.

If you play golf you already know that one of the great things about the game is that you cannot take your personal problems to the golf course. Golf requires total concentration. Just think, for four hours you have no other problem than your next golf swing. If everyone played golf a few times a week there would be less need for psychiatrists. Golfers who live in a climate where golf can be played the year around have a distinct advantage over those who do not.

There are times when I am sorry that golf handicaps have become so important at private clubs. I can remember many years ago when we did not need complicated handicap systems with course ratings and slope values for friendly competition. When we had a match we would give or take a certain number of strokes on each side or give a certain number on the front side and adjust after the ninth hole was played. My experience at the clubs where I have played is that a member was required to post an eighteen hole score every time that member played and there was a handicap committee to make sure that he did. I have no problem with turning in a scorecard. What I am sorry about is that these rigid requirements discourage golfers from playing better ball or foursome matches.

Both a four ball match, where a player can pick up his ball when he is out of the hole, and a two ball foursome match take less time to play. We could all play more golf if the game didn't take four hours or longer. The last time I played in Scotland I was very happy to see that two ball matches were still being played. I realize that handicaps are necessary for some club tournaments, but there should not be a requirement that scores be posted for every round. Golf is a game; it should be fun! More variety would make it more fun.

For a little nostalgia, I mentioned earlier that I was a Charter Member of the Golf Collectors Society. Every year this organization conducts a Hickory Hackers Tournament. At that time, perhaps clad in plus fours, members play an eighteen-hole tournament using wood-shafted golf clubs. By now these golf clubs are all at least seventy-five years old. In 1976 I was the winner of this event, my only international victory. The prize that I received for winning this prestigious tournament was a smooth-faced, hickory-shafted iron that was hand forged by Armstrong & Co. of Newcastle-on-Tyne, Scotland.

It seems that all of life is now one kind of competition or another. It starts in elementary school with grades and intensifies with competitions for athletic scholarships or grade point averages required for acceptance by prestigious universities. Everyone reading this knows how this continues for college students as they compete to make professional teams or to get good job offers. Is it any wonder that there are now so many adult recreational activities that are of a hazardous nature? I refer to sky diving and bungee jumping as examples. Golf is the opposite; so is fishing, and so is sailing. When I was young I enjoyed riding a motorcycle and I raced a hydroplane at the World's Fair that was held in Chicago in 1933. But all of that was before I was twenty years old.

It would be difficult to put into words just how much golf has meant to me, what a big a part of my life it has been. For more than eighty years I have been involved with golf in one way or another. Sometimes I feel guilty because I wish I had been able to give more back to this game that brought me so much pleasure. There were several years when I spent most Friday mornings during the golf season helping young boys and girls who participated in the junior golf program of the St. Louis District Golf Association. Also, after I retired I feel that I did make some contribution to the advancement of golf while I did consulting work for various firms in the San Diego area over a period of fifteen years. This was a win-win situation because the consulting work was great fun for me, too.

While I cannot be sure, I have a strong feeling that golf made a major contribution to both my physical and mental health. Golf always gave me something to look forward to and it constantly provided me with a challenge. At the age of 93, I am blessed with the kind of memory that is still good enough to recall all the things I wrote in this book. I can only wish the same pleasures and results for you.

APPENDIX ONE
TIMELINE OF SIGNIFICANT GOLF EVENTS

It is interesting to develop a time line, of sorts, that presents changes in the rules of golf and achievements by players that brought the game of golf to where it is at this point in time. Rather than go all the way back to the fifteenth century, this appendix will primarily deal with what has taken place during the last 100 years or so. It was about that time that club makers learned to make a socket-head wood and that scared-head woods disappeared from the golf course and resurfaced in golf collections. Another reason for starting the time line at this point is that golf really took hold in this country about 1895. Only a few of the events that occurred before 1895 will be included.

During the early years, golf was a gentleman's and lady's game. Yes, Mary, Queen of Scots, (French by birth), was an avid golfer. The golfing attire of the members of the Royal Order of Blackheath would befit a Revolutionary war General, tricorn hat and all. The players played the part in every way. The first organization, the forerunner to the USGA, was named The Amateur Golf Association of the United States. Only amateur golfers were permitted to enter the clubhouse through the front door of golf clubs. As with many other areas, such as automobiles, airplanes, etc., the rules of golf and golf equipment went through many changes during the twentieth century. The rules of golf were not responsible for golf equipment progress, but they did limit the use of some novel ideas, even patented inventions, on the platform of protecting the integrity of the game. One of the best events that finally took place was when the United States Golf Association and the Royal and Ancient Golf Society agreed to a common set of rules that covers golfers all over the world. For that we can all be grateful. Let us proceed with an abbreviated list of events and happenings that helped to shape the game of golf and the people that made it happen.

1618	The feather-stuffed golf ball is invented.
1743	The first golf publication, The Goff, is printed.
1764	St. Andrews golf course changed to 18 holes.
1826	Hickory wood is used for golf club shafts.
1848	The gutta perch ball is introduced.
1860	The British Open is born, and won by old Tom Morris.
1869	At the age of 17, young Tom Morris wins the first of four British Opens.
1873	The British Open is held at St. Andrews for the first time.
1888	The St. Andrews Golf Club is formed in New York.
1894	The British Open is played in England for the first time.
1894	The Amateur Golf Association of the United States is formed. The First American Golf Magazine , *The Golfer,* is published.
1895	First U.S. Amateur Championship held. First U.S. Open held the following day at 18 holes. Ten professionals and one amateur play in the event. Willie Anderson is the winner.
1898	Coburn Haskell patents rubber-wound ball. U.S. Open expanded to 36 holes.
1900	Harry Vardon is the first golfer to win both U.S. Open and the British Open.
1902	First irons built with grooves.
1903	Walter Travis wins British Amateur using center-shafted Schenectady putter.
1905	First dimple golf balls patented.
1906	Alex Smith wins U.S. Open and is the first man to break 300 in this event.
1907	Pinehurst No.2 course opens with 18 holes.
1909	Robert Gardner wins U.S. Amateur at age of 19. President Taft is the first U.S. president to play golf. USGA rules that caddies, caddy masters, and greenskeepers past the age of 16 are professionals.
1910	Patent for tubular steel golf shaft is issued. Steel shafts are deemed to be illegal.

R & A bans center-shafted putters.

USGA sets new values for par:

Par 3–Up to 225 yards

Par 4–226 to 425 yards

Par 5–426 to 600 yards

Par 6–601 yards and over

1912   John Ball wins eighth British Amateur.

1913   Francis Ouimet wins U.S. Open over Harry Vardon and Ted Ray.

1914   Harry Vardon wins his sixth British Open.

1916   Chick Evans, amateur, wins U.S. Open.

Bobby Jones plays in U.S. Amateur at age of fourteen.

Par yardage changed, again:

Par 3–Up to 250 yards

Par 4–251 to 445 yards

Par 5–446 to 600 yards

Par 6–More than 600 yards

PGA of America is formed. Jim Barnes wins the first PGA Championship.

1919   Pebble Beach Golf Links opens.

1920   USGA and R&A agree on standard ball: 1.62 inches in diameter and 1.62 ounces in weight.

1921   Jock Hutchinson wins British Open using deep-grooved irons.

1922   Walter Hagen is the first American-born golfer to win the British Open.

USGA Amateur Public Links Championship is inaugurated.

1923   Bobby Jones wins his first U.S. Open at age 21.

1924   Bobby Jones wins the first of five U.S. Amateur titles.

Steel shafts are approved for use by USGA, not by the R&A.

Bobby Jones wins both U.S. and British Opens.

Walter Hagen wins fourth successive PGA Championship.

1931   Billy Burke first to win U.S. Open using steel shafts.

U.S.G.A. increases ball size to 1.68 inches in diameter and reduces weight to 1.55 ounces.

1932   Gene Sarazen wins U.S. and British Opens.

Concave-faced sand wedge is banned.

Sarazen introduces flanged sand wedge.

1933   Augusta National Golf club founded.

1934   Lawson Little wins both USGA and British Amateurs for the first time.

Horton Smith wins first Augusta National Invitational.

Paul Runyan is leading money winner for year, with $6,767.

1935   Gene Sarazen makes double eagle on Augusta's 15th hole.

Glenna Collett Vare wins U.S. Womens Amateur for the 6th time.

1936   Johnny Fisher wins USGA Amateur using wood-shafted clubs.

1937   Sam Snead wins five tournaments in his first year.

U.S. Ryder Cup team wins in Great Britain for the first time.

1938   USGA limits players to fourteen clubs.

Sam Snead wins eight tournaments and earns $19,534.

1942   U.S. government stops manufacturing golf equipment due to war.

1942   Tam O'Shanter Open offers record purse of $42,000.

1945   Byron Nelson wins eleven successive tournaments and eighteen tournaments in all during the year.

1946   Ben Hogan wins thirteen PGA events.

First U.S. Women's Open is won by Patty Berg.

1947   First U.S.Open televised locally in St. Louis.

Babe Zaharias is the first American to win British Ladies Amateur.

1949   Louise Suggs wins U.S. Open by 14 strokes.

Ben Hogan critically injured in automobile accident.

1951   USGA and R&A agree on a set of uniform Rules of Golf with exception of golf ball size.

Stymie is abolished.

Center-shafted putters are legalized by R&A.

Golf Digest begins publishing.

Frances Ouimet becomes first American Captain of R & A.

1953   Ben Hogan wins all three majors that he enters.

First nationally-televised golf tournament: Tam O'Shanter World Championship.

1954   U.S. Open televised for the first time.

Gallery ropes are used for the first time at U.S. Open.

World championship has first $50,000 winner prize.

1955   USGA changes par distances:

Par 3–up to 250 yards

Par 4–251 to 470 yards

Par 5–471 yards and over

Mike Souchak shoots 27 under par for 72 holes: still a record.

1956   Masters Tournament televised for the first time.

1957   Great Britain wins Ryder Cup for first time in 24 years.

1958   PGA Championship changes from match to stroke play.

1959   Jack Nicklaus wins U.S. Amateur Championship.

Golf magazine begins publication.

1960   Rules changed to permit lifting, cleaning, and repairing ball marks on putting green.

1961   Mickey Wright wins three majors.

PGA of America drops Caucasian-only clause from its constitution.

1962   Jack Nicklaus wins his first U.S. Open at Oakmont.

Mickey Wright wins 10 tournaments for second successive year.

Water hazards are marked with painted lines.

1963   Arnold Palmer is first player to win $100,000 in a year.

Mickey Wright wins thirteen tournaments.

1964   Pete Brown, African American, wins an official PGA event.

Mickey Wright wins her 4th U.S. Women's Open and a total of 11 tournaments, shoots a record 62.

1965   Sam Snead wins his 82nd PGA Tour event. He wins the greater Greensboro Tournament for the 8th time.

U.S. Amateur changes from match to stroke play.

U.S. Open changes from three days to four days.

PGA Tour qualifying school started.

1967	Catherine Lacoste, of France, becomes first amateur to win U.S. Women's open.
1968	Croquet style putting is ruled illegal by USGA.
	Tournament Players Division created within the PGA.
	Trevino is first player to break 70 for all four rounds in a U.S. Open.
	Arnold Palmer becomes first player to win more than $1,000,000 in career earnings.
	Kathy Withworth and Carol Mann each win 10 tournaments on the LPGA Tour.
1971	Alan Shepard hits a six iron shot on the moon.
	Jack Nicklaus becomes first player to win all four majors twice.
1972	Spalding introduces the first two-piece golf ball.
1973	USGA Amateur returns to match play.
	Graphite shafts are introduced.
1975	Lee Elder is first African American to play in the Masters.
1976	USGA adopts the Overall Distance Standard for golf balls.
	Judy Rankin is first woman to earn more than $100,000 in one season.
1977	Al Geiberger is first PGA Tour player to break sixty, shooting 59 at Memphis.
	U.S. Open is first American golf event on television to cover all 18 holes.
1978	Nancy Lopez wins five tournaments in a row.
	Jack Nicklaus wins British Open for the 3rd time, giving him all four majors for the 3rd time.
	Legends of Golf, a new senior tour, is initiated.
1979	TaylorMade introduces its first metal wood.
	Sam Snead, at 67, shoots 66 during Quad City Open.
1980	USGA adds U.S. Senior Open to its list.
	USGA introduces golf ball "Symmetry Standard" to rules.
	1981 Kathy Whitworth is first woman golfer to win $1,000,000 in career earnings.
	USGA adds U.S. Mid-Amateur Championship.
1983	All-Exempt Tour instituted, eliminating Monday qualifying.

1985	USGA introduces the Slope System to adjust handicaps according to the difficulty of the course being played.
1986	Jack Nicklaus wins his sixth Masters Tournament.
	First $1,000,000 purse tournament held in Las Vegas.
1987	PGA Tour tops $30,000,000 in prize money.
1988	Curtis Strange becomes first player to earn $1,000,000 in one season.
	USGA rules that Ping irons do not conform to the Rules. Ping takes the USGA to court.
1989	PGA announces a ban on square grooves in irons. Ping wins a court injunction.
1990	PGA of America announces that it will no longer play any tournament at clubs that do not have African American members.
	R&A adopts American-sized ball (1.68 inches) as standard for the whole world.
	Ben Hogan Tour is initiated, later succeeded by Nike Tour.
1991	As an amateur, 20 year old Phil Mickelson wins PGA Tour event.
	Chip Beck shoots a 59 at Las Vegas.
1992	Ray Floyd wins on both PGA Tour and Senior Tour.
1993	Tiger woods wins U.S. Junior Amateur for 3rd straight year.
1996	Tiger Woods wins 3rd consecutive U.S. Amateur championship.
	Tiger Woods is named PGA Tour Rookie of the year.
	Annika Sorenstam wins second consecutive Women's Open Championship.
1997	Tiger Woods wins Masters Tournament by 12 strokes.
	Jack Nicklaus competes in his 150th consecutive major championship.
1999	USGA issues ruling on "trampoline effect."
2000	Michelle Wie, at 10, is the youngest player to compete in a USGA Women's Amateur Championship.
	Tiger Woods wins U.S. Open by 15 strokes.
	USGA celebrates 100th anniversary of U.S. Open, U.S., and U.S. Women's Amateur.
2001	Annika Sorenstam shoots 59 in an LPGA event.

2003   Michelle Wie at 13 wins the Women's Amateur Public Links Championship.

APPENDIX TWO
GOLF BALL VELOCITY AND
COEFFICIENT OF RESTITUTION

Two laws of physics are used to derive the equations employed in the analysis of Chapter Ten, the Principle of the Conservation of Momentum and the Principle of the Conservation of Energy.

Principle of Conservation of Momentum: *When no external forces are acting upon a body or system of bodies, the component linear momentum along any line and the angular momentum about any line remain constant.*

For a two-body system, such as clubhead and golf ball, this principle can be represented by the equation:

$$MU_1 + mU_2 = Mv_1 + mv_2 = (M+m)U_3 = \text{Constant} \qquad (1)$$

Principle of Conservation of Energy: *If a body or system of bodies is isolated so that it neither receives nor gives out energy, its total store of energy, all forms included, remains constant. There may be a transfer of energy from one part of the system to another, but the total gain or loss in one part is exactly equivalent to the loss or gain in the remainder.*

This principle is stated in equation form as follows:

$$\tfrac{1}{2} MU_1^2 + \tfrac{1}{2} mU_2^2 = \tfrac{1}{2} Mv_1^2 + \tfrac{1}{2} mv_2^2 = \text{Constant} \qquad (2)$$

Where: M = mass of the clubhead

m = mass of the golf ball (1.62 ounces)

U_1 = Clubhead velocity just prior to impact

U_2 = Golf ball velocity before impact = 0

U_3 = Average clubhead and golf ball velocity during impact

v_1 = Clubhead velocity just after separation

v_2 = Golf ball velocity just after separation

Since the ball is at rest before impact, the term $mU_2 = 0$ in Equation (1) for our example, we will use a clubhead weighing 205 grams (7.23 ounces) with an impact velocity of 100 mph. then since

$$MU_1 = (M + m)U_3$$

$$U_3 = MU_1 / M+m$$

$$U_3 = U_1 / (1+m/M)$$

$$U_3 = 100/1.224 = 81.7 \text{ mph}$$

This tells us that during the half millisecond of contact the clubhead and the ball have an average velocity of 81.7 mph.

If we divide Equation (2) by the first two parts of Equation (1) and simplify, we obtain

$$(v_2-v_1)/U_1-U_2) = 1$$

The numerator in this equation represents the difference between the velocities of the ball and the clubhead after impact, and the denominator represents the difference between the velocities of the clubhead and ball prior to impact. The two relative velocities must be equal if kinetic energy is conserved. However, since the golf ball is deformed during impact, kinetic energy cannot be conserved and the ratio of the two relative velocities becomes the Coefficient of Restitution, symbolized by "e" or COR. Since $U_2 = 0$,

$$e = (v_2-v_1)/ U_1 \qquad\qquad (3)$$

COR always has a value between 0 and 1.0. From Equation (3)

$$v_1 = v_2-eU_1$$

If we substitute this value of v1 into Equation (1), "e" can be expressed in a more useful form

$$e = [v_2 (1+ m/M)/U_1]-1 \qquad\qquad (4)$$

In a typical example from driver tests using 90 compression balls at clubhead speeds of 100mph, the initial golf ball velocity was measured at 212.5 fps or 144.8 mph. In this case, using a 205 gram clubhead,

$$e = (144.8 \times 1.224)/100\text{-}1 = 0.77$$

This value of "e" will be used below as appropriate.

Now we are in a position to calculate the initial golf ball velocity, which occurs immediately after separation from the clubhead. This will be done for both the ideal, perfectly elastic ball (e = 1.00) and the actual golf ball (e = 0.77) From equation (4)

$$v_2 = U_1 (1+e)/(1+m/M)$$

Using our example golf club,

For the ideal golf ball with e = 1.00

$$v_2 = (100 \times 2) /1.224 = 163 \text{ mph} = 240 \text{ fps.}$$

For a golf ball with e = 0.77

$$v_2 = 100 \times 1.770)/1.224 = 144.6 \text{ mph} = 212 \text{ fps}$$

Note that the only difference in initial golf ball velocity and the actual ball is only 11.7 percent.

It is now possible to calculate the velocity of the clubhead (v_1) immediately after impact for both the perfectly elastic ball and the actual compressible golf ball of our example. From the equation for "e"

$$v_1 = v_2\text{-} eU_1$$

When e = 1.00 $\qquad\qquad v_1 = 163\text{–}100 = 63 \text{ mph}$

When e = 0.77 $\qquad\qquad v_1 = 145\text{–}77 = 68 \text{ mph}$

In summary, we can safely say that the modern golf ball is a remarkable device with its COR of 0.77 for a 90 compression ball. It is even higher for the 100 compression ball. All of the above calculations are based upon using a driver with a rigid face. This means that all of the energy loss takes place in the ball and there is no energy loss in the clubhead. The case of the thin-face driver was discussed elsewhere.

APPENDIX THREE
FORCE CREATED DURING IMPACT

Assume:

U = 110 mph = 161.4 fps = clubhead velocity

M = 205 grams = 7.23 oz. = 0.452 lbs. = clubhead weight.

M = 45.9 grams = 1.62 oz. = 0.101 lbs = weight of ball

e = 0.77 Coefficient of Restitution

g = 32.17 ft/sec^2 acceleration due to gravity

v_2 – Initial golf ball velocity

The equation for the initial velocity of a golf ball (immediately after impact) can be derived by employing two of the basic laws of physics as demonstrated in APPENDIX ONE.

This is expressed as

v_2 = U(1+e)/1+(m/M)

Using the assumed values

v_2 = 161.4(1+0.77)/ 1 +(1.62/7.23)

v_2 = 161.4 x 1.077/1.224

v_2 = 233 fps (initial golf ball velocity)

Average force during impact, from Newton's Second Law

F_{avg} = mass x acceleration

F_{avg} = ma = m x dv/dt

It has been established by experiment that the duration of contact between the clubhead and the ball in a central impact situation (driver) is approximately one-half millisecond (0.0005 sec).

Therefore F_{avg} = (0.101/32.17) x (233–0)/0.0005 = 1463 pounds

This is the average force during impact. The peak force is approximately forty percent greater than the average force, or more than 2000 pounds.

1   (The Rules of Golf as revised by the Royal and Ancient Golf Club of St. Andrews in 1891 with rulings and interpretations by the Executive Committee of The United States Golf Association in 1897. The Official Golf Guide for 1891, Spalding Athletic Library.)